I0617502

From Farmland
to Card Shop

A History of Shadyside
Through the Windows of 5522 Walnut St.

Author: Jason Kirin
Editor: Dana Kaufman

ISBN: 979-8-9878496-5-1 (Paperback)
ISB: 979-8-9878496-0-6 (Full Color Large Print)
ISBN: 979-8-9878496-1-3 (Digital)

Front cover design and layout by: Jason Kirin

Self-published through IngramSpark

First printed edition: June 2022
Second printed edition: March 2024

Introduction..5

Part One: Early History.............................. 8

Part Two: Residential History......................... 13

   George Gibson.....................................16

   The Benzenhoefers..............................18

   Barbara Stannard.................................26

   J.B. Nimmick... 32

   Fred Younghurtz....................................33

   Joseph and Edward Krumm....................34

   Joseph Shafer, Frank Zangrilli, Orpha Priscilla
   Zangrilli... 38

   Honorable Mentions..............................39

Part Three: Commercial History.....................41

   Barbershop, Beauty Parlor,
   Patent Article Manufacturer
   1893 - 1940...45

   Dimling & Cable Inc. Interior Designers
   1955 - 1962...46

   Dr. Daniel Kaufman
   1946 - 1958...50

   The Village Treat Shop
   1962 - 1964...52

   Papa Joe's
   1964 - 1974...53

   Adam's Rib Room
   1976..56

   The Hollywood Social Club
   1948 - 1982...57

   Every Cloud Has a Dynamic Lining
   (Time to Embrace Change ... Barbara)............... 73

Kards Unlimited
1957/1974 - Present Day.............................78

   Shopping with Polly

1927.. 80
Kards Unlimited
A Modern Legacy.................................. 85
Afterward.. **95**
Acknowledgements.. **98**
Archivist / Archive Acknowledgments.................... **109**
Digital / Online Archive..................................**111**
Contact and Social Media Info..................**116**
Endnotes..**117**

Introduction

In May of 2022, I began a research project regarding the life of my maternal grandmother, Shirley Cavanaugh. I purchased a membership to *Newspapers.com* and started collecting articles that mentioned her. As I sat, scouring the archives, a thought occurred to me... My wife's birthday was approaching; could I find something in these archives that would serve well as a gift? After all, I knew the building where her business is located has some history to it. During the 1950s, there was an after-hours speakeasy called the Hollywood Social Club and I knew, at some point, the mob was even involved with ownership. Certainly I could find something, an article or maybe a photograph I could colorize and restore. Either way, I knew my grandmother would have to wait. In the search bar of *Newspapers.com* I typed "5522 Walnut St."

In seconds, 169 archived newspapers loaded, chronologically, before me. Confused, I sat for a moment, staring at the first result: *The Pittsburgh Press*, Wednesday April 12th, 1893. Surely that couldn't be correct. The first mention of 5522 Walnut St. in a newspaper was *129 years ago*?

LOST—Irish setter dog; answers to name of Chief. Reward if returned to 5522 Walnut st., Shady Side, Pittsburg. 411MY

Pittsburgh Press Monday March 31, 1941.

Soon it was apparent that 5522 Walnut St. was a home. A house with a front and rear address separated by a yard. People lived and loved within its walls as early as the 1890s and as recently as the 1940s. Businesses opened and closed their doors across the decades. In 1948, a man named Frank Blandi purchased the rear address and built a two-story extension across the yard to create the Hollywood Social Club, ultimately conjoining the front and rear address into the single structure where Kards Unlimited is located today.

Reading through these articles warmly knit the tapestry of space and time together around my heart. A warp and weft of unbroken threads stretching as far back as 1868 began to unspool within me. There was magic here. There was love. There was death. But most importantly, there is a community spanning generations that stretches the entire reach of Walnut St.

Here that history is stitched together by newspaper clippings, uncovered photographs, ancestry research, and narrative histories that have been woven by the threads of Shadyside's history.

The weaving of which is a gift to my wife — Amanda Blair.

Jason Kirin 6/22

Part One: Early History

We begin in 1868, when the city of Pittsburgh absorbed a farm owned by Rachel Aiken and her cousin-husband, Thomas Aiken. Apparently the land's pleasantness inspired the Shadyside name.

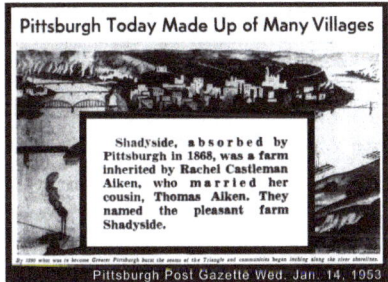

Pittsburgh Today Made Up of Many Villages

Shadyside, absorbed by Pittsburgh in 1868, was a farm inherited by Rachel Castleman Aiken, who married her cousin, Thomas Aiken. They named the pleasant farm Shadyside.

Pittsburgh Post Gazette Wed. Jan. 14, 1953

Moving on into 1872, as plots and properties began to grow borders, a series of commonly known Pittsburgh names began to grace the pages of these historically archived maps.

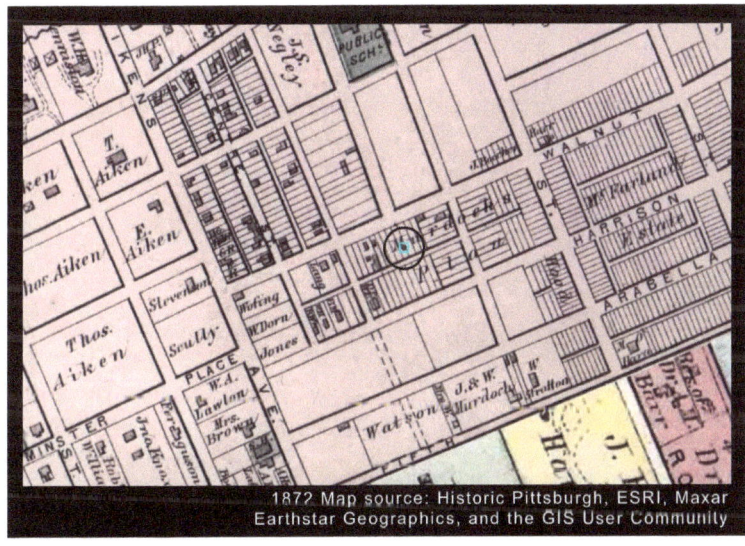

1872 Map source: Historic Pittsburgh, ESRI, Maxar Earthstar Geographics, and the GIS User Community

Names such as Murdock, an early Pittsburgh family who, since 1840, had been homesteading in and around Squirrel Hill. This section of Murdock's Plan became another one of their properties.

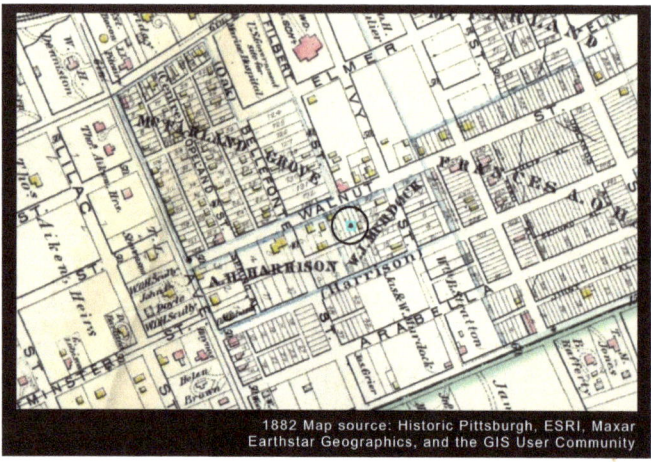

1882 Map source: Historic Pittsburgh, ESRI, Maxar
Earthstar Geographics, and the GIS User Community

Then, between 1882 and 1890, Murdock's Plan was sold to philanthropist William Thaw, a businessman who made his fortune in transportation, banking, and property ownership. He purchased lots 32 and 33 of Murdock's Plan.

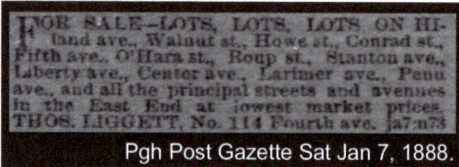

FOR SALE—LOTS, LOTS, LOTS ON Highland ave., Walnut st., Howe st., Conrad st., Fifth ave., O'Hara st., Roup st., Stanton ave., Liberty ave., Center ave., Larimer ave., Penn ave., and all the principal streets and avenues in the East End at lowest market prices. THOS. LIGGETT, No. 114 Fourth ave. ja7;n73

Pgh Post Gazette Sat Jan 7, 1888.

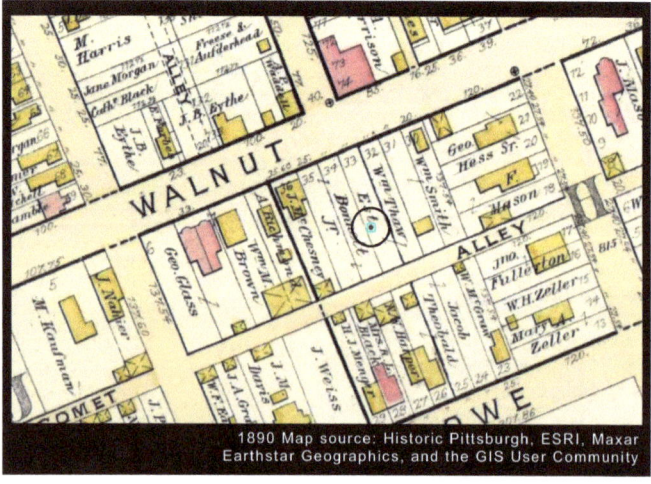

1890 Map source: Historic Pittsburgh, ESRI, Maxar
Earthstar Geographics, and the GIS User Community

Interestingly, Thaw's grandson, Lt. Colonel William Thaw II, was one of, if not the first, American to engage in aerial combat in WW1 and, with five confirmed aerial kills, Thaw held the title of "Flying-Ace."

At some point, he and his squadron pooled their funds together to purchase a lion as a mascot – they named it Whiskey. [1]

Then they bought a second one... and named it Soda.

By 1890, Emil Sitz became the owner of both lot 32 and 33. In December of 1890, Sitz was granted a permit to build a brick, two-story home with a mansard dwelling on the third floor. In 1892, Sitz sold this house to John J. Benzenhoefer. Now plot 33 had become a home. A home that was given the address...

...5522 Walnut Street, Pittsburg Pa.

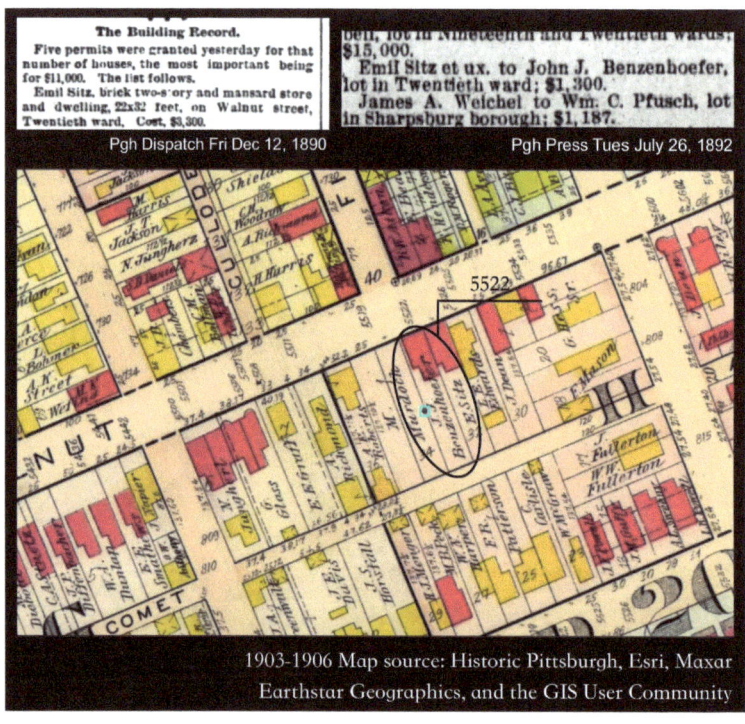

1903-1906 Map source: Historic Pittsburgh, Esri, Maxar Earthstar Geographics, and the GIS User Community

Part Two: Residential History

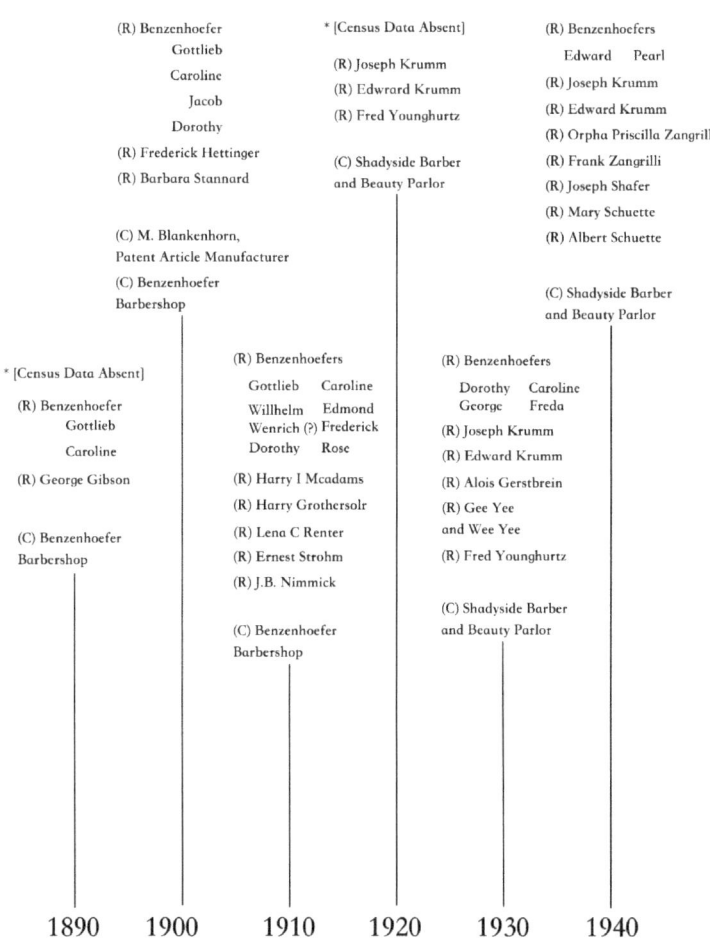

(R) Benzenhoefer
Gottlieb
Caroline
Jacob
Dorothy
(R) Frederick Hettinger
(R) Barbara Stannard

(C) M. Blankenhorn,
Patent Article Manufacturer
(C) Benzenhoefer
Barbershop

* [Census Data Absent]
(R) Joseph Krumm
(R) Edwrard Krumm
(R) Fred Younghurtz

(C) Shadyside Barber
and Beauty Parlor

(R) Benzenhoefers
Edward   Pearl
(R) Joseph Krumm
(R) Edward Krumm
(R) Orpha Priscilla Zangrilli
(R) Frank Zangrilli
(R) Joseph Shafer
(R) Mary Schuette
(R) Albert Schuette

(C) Shadyside Barber
and Beauty Parlor

* [Census Data Absent]
(R) Benzenhoefer
Gottlieb
Caroline
(R) George Gibson

(C) Benzenhoefer
Barbershop

(R) Benzenhoefers
Gottlieb   Caroline
Willhelm   Edmond
Wenrich (?) Frederick
Dorothy   Rose
(R) Harry I Mcadams
(R) Harry Grothersolr
(R) Lena C Renter
(R) Ernest Strohm
(R) J.B. Nimmick

(C) Benzenhoefer
Barbershop

(R) Benzenhoefers
Dorothy   Caroline
George   Freda
(R) Joseph Krumm
(R) Edward Krumm
(R) Alois Gerstbrein
(R) Gee Yee
and Wee Yee
(R) Fred Younghurtz

(C) Shadyside Barber
and Beauty Parlor

1890   1900   1910   1920   1930   1940

*1890 Census Data lost to fire in 1921
1920 Census taker skipped 5522 Walnut St.

1890 & 1920 information garnered from
newspaper archives, museum archives and
ancestry research.

Three things must be noted regarding the US Census information.

First, tragically, the 1890 US Population Census was almost entirely destroyed by fire and water damage in 1921. [1]

Second, unfortunately, the 1920 Census data taker simply skipped 5522 Walnut St. altogether.

Third, luckily, 5522 Walnut St. was only residential from the 1890s until the 1940s, and the census information for 1900, 1910, 1930, and 1940 were easily accessible.

When intertwined from available census data, ancestry research, and newspaper archives, we see vignettes of the tenants' lives painted momentarily back into reality.

We're allowed a glimpse of moments that have passed in shared spaces that have transcended time.

George Gibson

As mentioned, the 1890 US Census was almost entirely lost to fire and water damage in 1921. Hence, our first resident is gleaned through experiences recorded in newspapers and other public documentation.

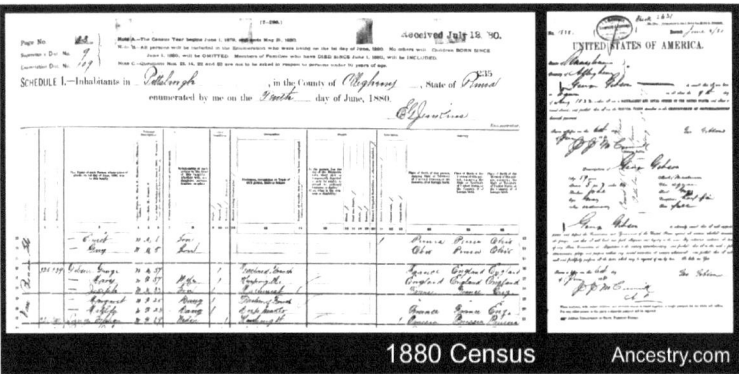

1880 Census   Ancestry.com

Having emigrated from France to Pittsburgh in 1881, George Gibson first took up residence at 325 Van Braam St. where, according to the 1880 census, he listed his occupation as Teacher of French.

Gibson was identified as a resident due to his death notice, which listed his address as 5522 Walnut St.

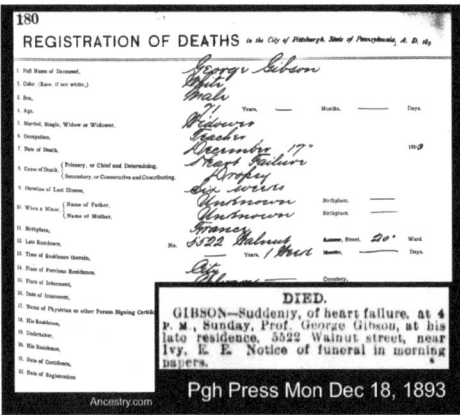

DIED.

GIBSON—Suddenly, of heart failure, at 4 P. M., Sunday, Prof. George Gibson, at his late residence, 5522 Walnut street, near Ivy, E. E. Notice of funeral in morning papers.

Pgh Press Mon Dec 18, 1893

Interestingly, it wasn't until the death notice of Gibson's daughter, Marguerite, in 1908, that we learn he was a professor at the Pennsylvania College for Women, which changed its name in 1957 to Chatham — which possibly made his move from Van Braam St. to Walnut St. a matter of walking convenience.

Mayor David Lawrence and Jane Burfoot mark the occasion of changing the name from Pa College for Women to Chatham College.
Source: Chatham University Chronological Photograph Files

Mrs. Edward F. Houston Dead.

Mrs. Marguerite Gibson Houston, wife of Edward F. Houston, secretary of D. P. Reighard, died suddenly at her home, 5515 Alder street, of heart failure, at 6:30 o'clock Wednesday morning. She had apparently been in excellent health and she had been nursing her husband, who has been in poor health for the past 10 days. Her death came as a great shock to her family and relatives. Mrs. Houston was the daughter of the late Prof. George Gibson, who was formerly connected with the Pennsylvania College for Women. She was born in La Rochelle, France, and came to this country when a child. Prior to her marriage, October 3, 1884, she assisted her father in teaching French literature, in which she was well versed. She is survived by three sons, Edward, George and Thomas Houston; one daughter, Marie Bell Houston, and a sister, Miss Matilda Gibson of the East End. She was a prominent member of the Roman Catholic church of the Sacred Heart. Funeral services will be held from the church at 9:30 o'clock this morning, when a solemn high mass will be celebrated by the Rev. Father Frances R. Karie.

Pgh Post Gazette Fri Oct 16, 1908

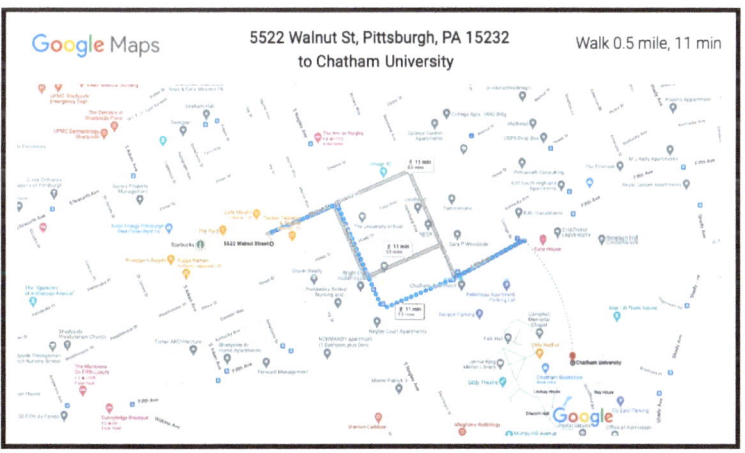

The Benzenhoefers

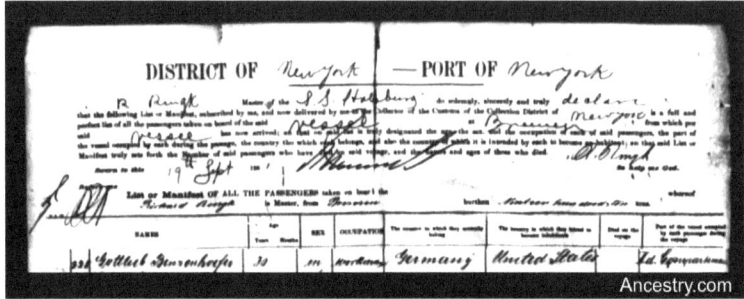

Ancestry.com

In 1881, Gottlieb Benzenhoefer arrived in New York City on a boat set out from Germany.[1] Although the next 10 years of Gottlieb's life are opaque, he ultimately moved to Pittsburgh around 1893.

Pittsburgh City Directories 1893-1899

---

[1] According to an article on http://www.norwayheritage.com/ this journey would have taken Gottlieb approximately nine days.

Contending with the information lost when the 1890 census was destroyed in a 1921 fire, we turn our attention to the R.L. Polk & Company Pittsburgh City Directories – most of which are available to peruse at the Detre Library & Archives at the Heinz History Center.

From these directories, we can verify that, during the 1890s, not only did Gottlieb live at 5522 Walnut St., but he also ran his business as a barber out of the same address.

Furthermore, an 1896 Marriage License Docket had both Gottlieb and his spouse Caroline Hilkert listed as living at the Benzenhoefer family home at 5522 Walnut St.

Caroline & Gottlieb Benzenhoefer

From the 1900 Census, no fewer than five Benzenhoefers lived at 5522 Walnut St.

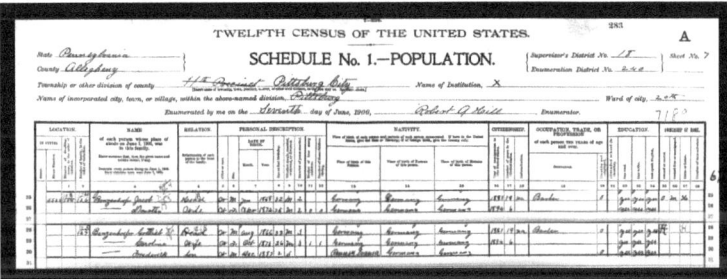

From the 1910 Census, we see that number climb to eight.

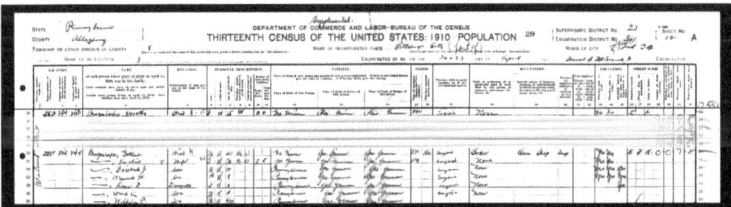

From the 1930 Census, we see that number move down to four.

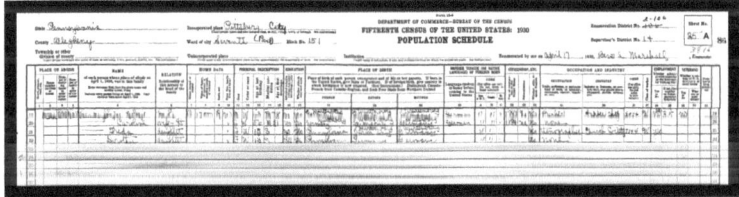

By the 1940s, only Edward and Pearl Benzenhoefer remained as Walnut St. began to commercialize further.

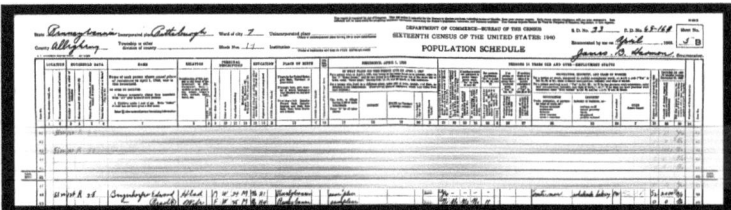

During those years…

A tragedy occurred on March 15th, 1912:

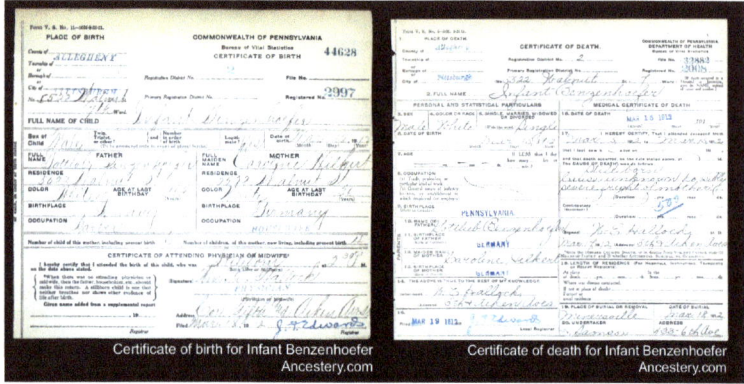

Certificate of birth for Infant Benzenhoefer
Ancestery.com

Certificate of death for Infant Benzenhoefer
Ancestery.com

In 1913 … life.

Certificate of birth for Freda Benzenhoefer
Ancestery.com

22

In 1931 … love.

Miss Freda Benzenhoefer Weds Mr. Guy M. Beaty In Pittsburgh

Young Couple to Make Trip Through North and in Florida Before Coming to Charlotte to Make Their Home.

A wedding of cordial interest to a wide circle of friends in this city was that of Miss Freda Benzenhoeffer of Pittsburgh, Pa., and Guy M. Beaty, Jr., of this city, which was solemnized last Saturday evening at the home of the bride's parents, Mr. and Mrs. G. Benzenhoeffer, at 5522 Walnut street, Pittsburgh, Pa.

The bride was given in marriage by her father and the bridegroom had as his best man Ed Benzenhoeffer, brother of the bride.

Rev. A G. Merkins, of the Lutheran church, pastor of the bride, officiated.

The bride was attired in light blue taffeta and carried a white Bible that was given her by her parents when she was confirmed. Her only ornament was a star pendant a gift of the bridegroom.

Relatives and a few intimate friends attended the wedding which was followed by a charming and informal reception.

The young couple left for a trip through the north and will later visit Florida after which they will be at home in Charlotte.

The bride was educated in the Pittsburgh school and is a bright and accomplished young woman. She was secretary to Dr. W. C. Chappell of the Pittsburgh Baptist association. She has been active in young peoples work in the Lutheran church and secretary of the Sunday school.

The bridegroom is the son of Mr. and Mrs. Guy M. Beaty of this city. He was educated in the city schools and specialized in mechanical engineering at Carnegie Tech at Pittsburgh. He is associated in business with his father contractor-distributor of pipe and boiler coverings in this city.

The Charlotte Observer Friday, July 3, 1931

23

Ultimately, Gottlieb died in 1937 and Caroline joined him, 364 days later, in 1938.

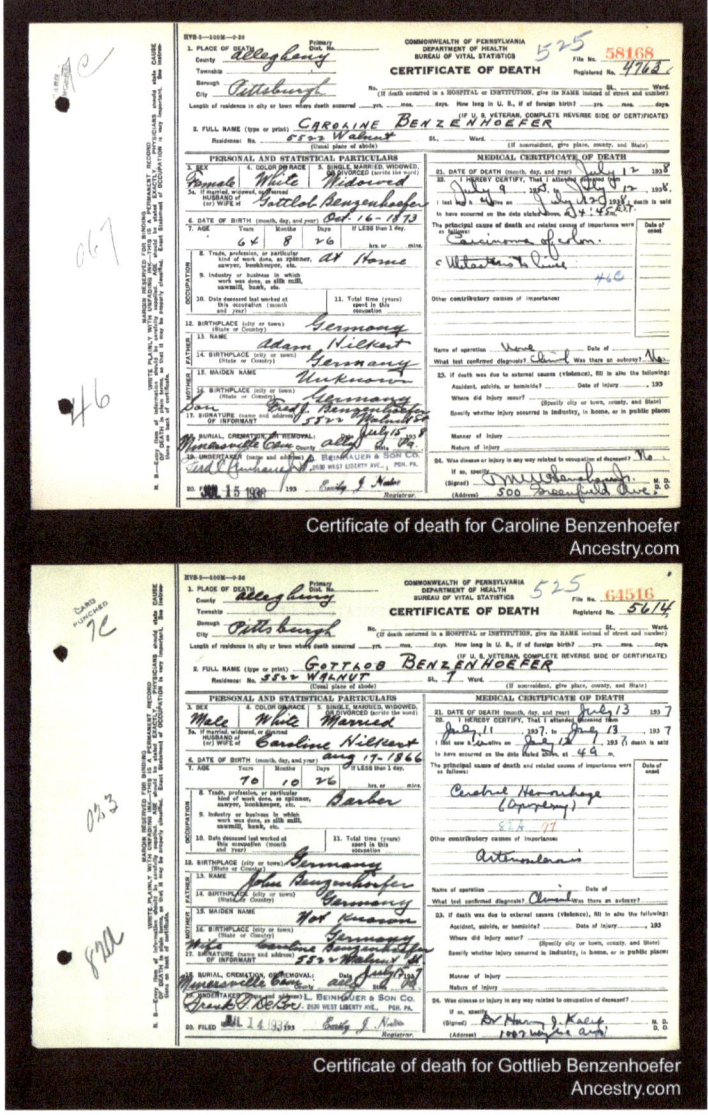

Certificate of death for Caroline Benzenhoefer
Ancestry.com

Certificate of death for Gottlieb Benzenhoefer
Ancestry.com

---

[2] The misspelling Gottlob was pervasive and ended up being the name on his gravestone.

I often think about Caroline and Gottlieb. The lives they must have lived under the same roof, between the same walls I find myself so often living. I stand near the poetry books, I draw my fingers along the shelf, I hear the floorboards creak beneath me. The same floorboards I know they too walked across. I'm not entirely certain how I feel about ghosts. I know little about spirits. I know, however, they are still here. A part of them remains. A part of them lives on in Kards Unlimited.

The Benzenhoefer Family at 5522 Walnut St. in 1908
contrasted against 5522 Walnut St. in 2022
Photo source: Ancestry.com

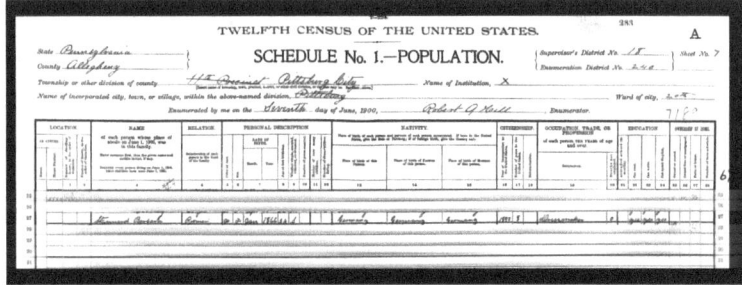

According to the 1900 Census, Barbara Stannard was a 34-year-old roomer. While she lived at 5522 Walnut St., she worked as a dressmaker.

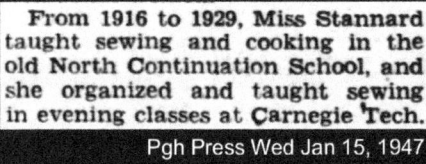

From 1916 to 1929, Miss Stannard taught sewing and cooking in the old North Continuation School, and she organized and taught sewing in evening classes at Carnegie Tech.

Pgh Press Wed Jan 15, 1947

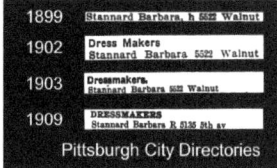

Pittsburgh City Directories

Stannard also taught night classes in dressmaking and costuming at Carnegie Tech. Moreover, she taught sewing and cooking at the North Continuation School.

She lived and worked at 5522 Walnut St. as a personalized dressmaker and, by the 1900s, Barbara opened her own dress shop on 5th Ave.

University Course in London.

In the spring of the same year she went to London, where she pursued a university course in English, literature and history. Upon returning to America last year most of her time was spent in writing for various Eastern magazines. Miss Bray arrived in Pittsburgh yesterday and assumes her work at once.

Miss Elizabeth Vermorcken has been appointed instructor in History. Miss Vermocken belongs to one of the oldest Pittsburgh families, has always lived here, and her literary work, of a high class, deals with educational and sociological questions.

Miss Barbara Stannard has been appointed instructor in the dressmaking department. Miss Stannard is of Polish descent, having received her education in Europe and has had years of valuable experience in her specialty. She is located in Pittsburgh and last year substituted for a short time in the night classes.

Pgh Daily Post Tues Sept 13, 1910

27

In her spare time as a teacher at Carnegie Tech, Barbara Stannard studied architecture. By the 1920s, she designed and built the first corrugated iron house in Pittsburgh. There she retired to not only take up painting and canary raising, but also followed her childhood love for bees, and created a small apiary sanctuary for a colony of 525,000 (sometimes depressed and grumbling) bees.

Here's 'Bee Line' Five Miles Long

A retired teacher of Pittsburg has 525.000 pets.

They are the bees she has tended for 15 years. If someone were patient enough and sufficiently cautious to place them they would make a line about five miles long.

A depression, it seems, has hit the bees and they grumble about it, according to Miss Barbara R. Stannard of 700 Graphic Street. The long spells of rain this spring kept the bees indoors, preventing them from collecting honey from fruit blossoms.

"When I was a little girl in Germany," Miss Stannard said, "I was given a book of bee stories. I have been studying them ever since, more than 60 years.

"I don't try to make any money from my bees. I love them and just keep them for pets."

Pgh Press Sun July 26, 1931

KEEPER OF THE BEES

MISS BARBARA R. STANNRAD—Fearlessly handling a swarm of bees outside her home in Greenfield. Miss Stannard is 72, one of the hundreds of beekeepers in Allegheny County.

Pgh Sun Telegraph Mon Nov 8, 1937

OLDEST KEEPER HERE

"Clustering" at the moment are the bees of Miss Barbara R. Stannard, Pittsburgh's oldest woman beekeeper. At her home at 700 Graphic Street, Greenfield, 71-year-old Miss Stannard has 10 colonies. Honey produced by her bees won a prize at the recent Allegheny County Fair. Active for her age, Miss Stannard still tends her bees and extracts the honey herself. However, she is seeking a buyer for her apiary because she is no longer able to care for the bees as she wishes. Her new interest is canary birds which she raises and sells.

Miss Stannard's interest in bees dates back to a child's illustrated bee book. But it wasn't until she installed her own beeyard in 1912 that she got a closeup of a bee. She explains why she took up beekeeping:

"Beekeeping is one way to 'Live Alone and Like It.' Having something to do is a way to forget your troubles. Too, bees provide an interesting study and bee behavior is something unusual. I would like to keep them but while the spirit is willing the body is wearing out."

Several brothers and sisters reside in the United States and she sees them "once in a while," but she says she will continue to live alone, baking her own bread, reading, writing and tending to her bees and canaries.

ALSO AN ARTIST

Too, she is doing a little drawing and painting. Last winter, she took a few drawing lessons and is offering encouragement to several youngsters who would like to become artists.

Pgh Sun Telegraph
Mon Nov 8, 1937

29

She came to Pittsburgh in 1897, organized and taught sewing in evening classes at Carnegie Tech and in between times studied architecture. The latter led to the erection of the first corrugated iron home in the city. It was prefabricated in St. Paul along lines designated by the little old lady who a neighbor described as: "Kind and considerate to all."

Harrisburg Telegraph
Thurs, Jan16, 1947

Barbara Stannard died January 11th, 1947. In her will, she decreed her entire estate (two dwellings and a lot equalling $12,000) be left to "assist fatherless girls in securing vocational or other educational training to help them support themselves." She also left her seven canaries (only three of them good singers, mind you) to the neighborhood insurance collector. Her apiary was to be moved to the Saint Barnabas Home.

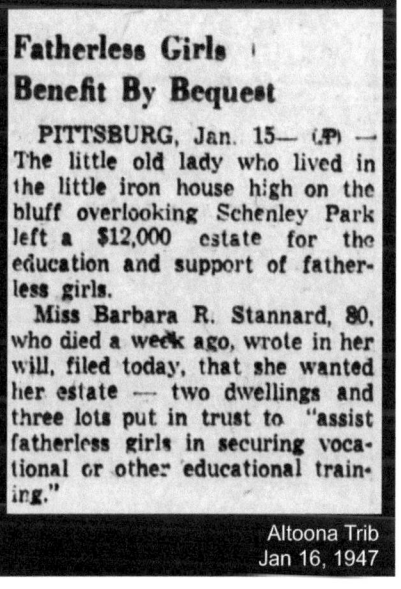

The Indiana Gazette
Wednesday, December 4, 1912

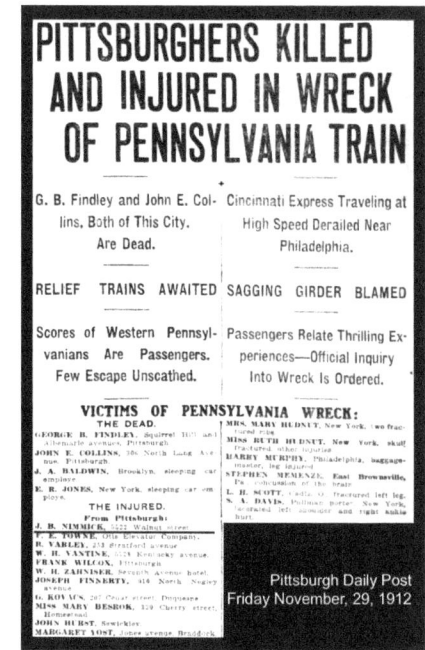

Pittsburgh Daily Post
Friday November, 29, 1912

A Pittsburgher injured in the 1912 Glenloch, Pennsylvania trainwreck, J.B. Nimmick was interesting and also complicated; the only accounts of the name J.B. Nimmick I found were in relation to this trainwreck in 1912. In only one article their address was mentioned as 5522 Walnut St. No census information. Nothing to cross reference.

Fred Younghurtz

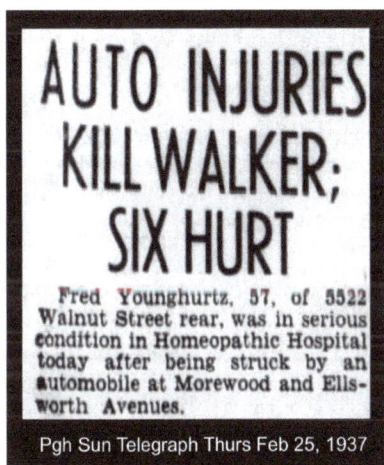

AUTO INJURIES KILL WALKER; SIX HURT

Fred Younghurtz, 57, of 5522 Walnut Street rear, was in serious condition in Homeopathic Hospital today after being struck by an automobile at Morewood and Ellsworth Avenues.

Pgh Sun Telegraph Thurs Feb 25, 1937

While neither spelling Younghurtz nor Jungherz appeared on any census records, there were two references to a Fred Younghurtz who took up residence at 5522 Walnut St. One was an account of him being a grocer, and the other of a car accident in which he was injured.

1921 - ONE OF THE FINEST AMBULANCES IN PGH.

Photos Source: Shadyside Hospital Records, 1852-2008, MSS 1203, Detre Library and Archives, Heinz History Center

Younghurtz was taken to the Homeopathic Hospital in 1937, which would change its name one year later to the Shadyside Hospital and then, 59 years later, become UPMC Shadyside.

Joseph and Edward Krumm

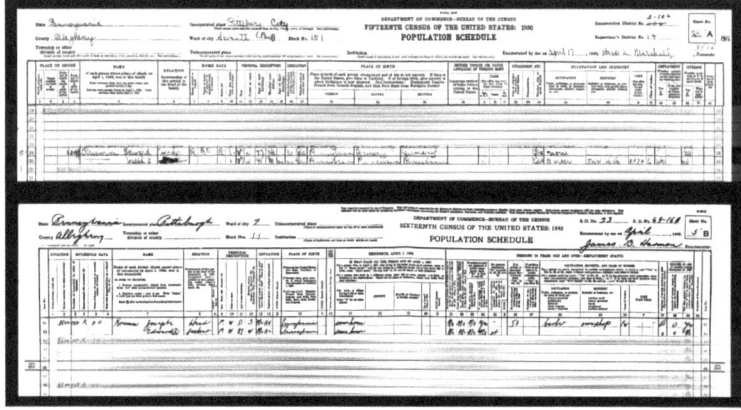

The Krumms were especially interesting, because the more information that was available, the more I was left with questions and less with answers.

Available census data, starting in 1860, allows us to follow Edward Krumm from the age of 8 until his eventual death at the age of 88.

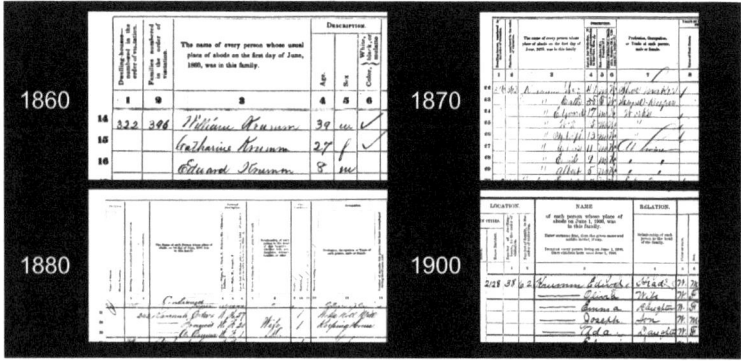

His father was a shoemaker named William. By the age of 17, Edward was listed on the 1870 census as a "worker." By 1880, Edward was married to Francis Olivia Krumm, and together they had a son, Joseph....

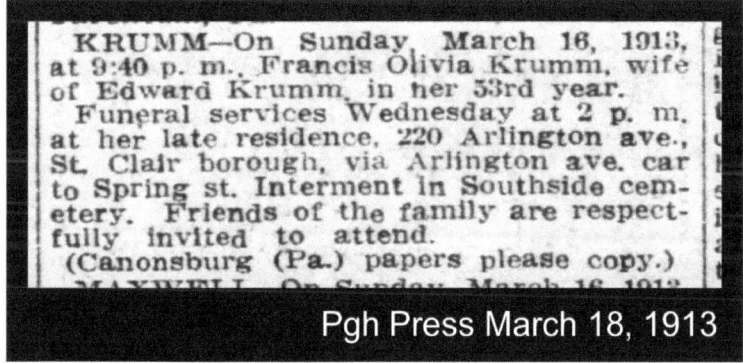

KRUMM—On Sunday, March 16, 1913, at 9:40 p. m., Francis Olivia Krumm, wife of Edward Krumm, in her 53rd year.
Funeral services Wednesday at 2 p. m. at her late residence, 220 Arlington ave., St. Clair borough, via Arlington ave. car to Spring st. Interment in Southside cemetery. Friends of the family are respectfully invited to attend.
(Canonsburg (Pa.) papers please copy.)

Pgh Press March 18, 1913

Francis Krumm died in 1913. By 1900, 47-year-old Edward's occupation was listed as "iron worker" and Joseph was in school. I was unable to uncover a 1910 Census record for Krumm and, as mentioned earlier, the 1920s Census taker skipped 5522 Walnut St. With information gathered from newspaper archives, I pieced together the following.

CANOE—State condition and price. Write J. E. Krumm, 5522 Walnut st., East End. 320wb

Pgh Press Sun March 20, 1921

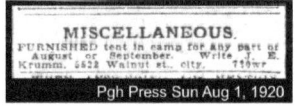

MISCELLANEOUS.
FURNISHED tent in camp for any part of August or September. Write J. E. Krumm, 5522 Walnut st., city. 710wr

Pgh Press Sun Aug 1, 1920

Joseph took an interest in canoeing and camping. He took out a few ads in search of an affordable canoe and soon thereafter began to place multiple items for sale in the same paper...

BOATS, YACHTS, ETC.

WANTED—Sponson canoe. Write J. Krumm, 5522 Walnut st., city.
919w

Pgh Press Sun Sept 19, 1920

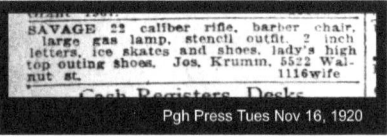

SAVAGE 22 caliber rifle, barber chair, large gas lamp, stencil outfit, 2 inch letters, ice skates and shoes, lady's high top outing shoes. Jos. Krumm, 5522 Walnut st. 1116wife

Pgh Press Tues Nov 16, 1920

A Savage .22 caliber rifle, barber chair, large gas lamp, stencil outfit, two-inch letters, ice skates, and lady's high top outing shoes.

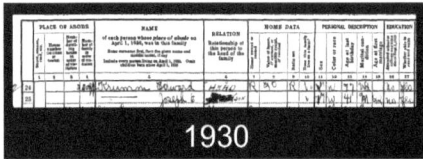

1930

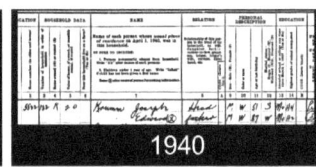

1940

The 1930 census revealed Edward Krumm, age 77, was still the head of house, and Joseph was still a barber. The 1940 Census indicated by the ⊠ next to Edward Krumm's name that he was the person who gave the information that day. Joseph was then the head of the house. At 87, Edward was not long for this world.

On March 30th, 1941, Edward Krumm died from a concussion he suffered 20 days earlier. According to the *Pittsburgh Press*, Krumm "stepped from the kitchen of his home into the rear yard March 10 and fell down one step, suffering the injury which caused his death."

When I looked at the Penn Pilot Program's 1939 Aerial Photographs of Shadyside, it was interesting to see the single structure standing at the front of Walnut St. with the long, empty corridor heading back toward Ivy St.

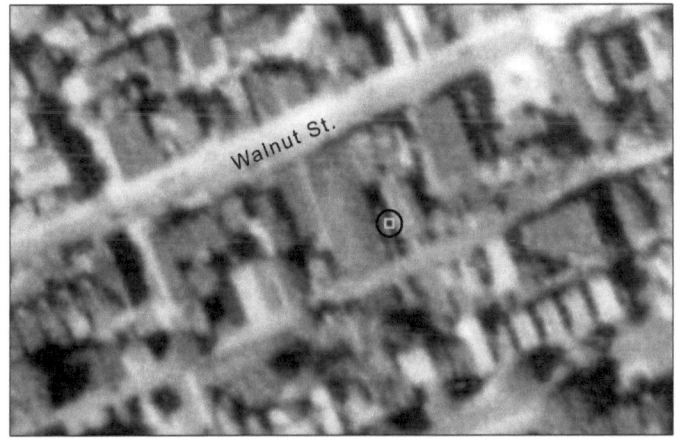

Fall Leads to Death

A fall down one step proved fatal to Edward Krumm, 88, of 5522 Walnut St., East End, who died in his home last night of a brain concussion. According to a report to the coroner, Mr. Krumm stepped from the kitchen of his home into the rear yard March 10 and fell down one step, suffering the injury which caused his death.

Pittsburgh Press Monday March 31, 1941.

Walnut St.

Penn Pilot Program's 1939 Aerial Photograph

I considered where, inside of Kards Unlimited, this "yard" must have been.

I assume it was near calendars, puzzles, and journals.

Perhaps Krumms and the Benzenhoefers are the friendly ghosts who wander about, adding charm and creakiness to the atmosphere of the store.

Both Joseph Shafer and Frank Zangrilli's WWII draft cards showed up in a search and have interestingly conflicting information.

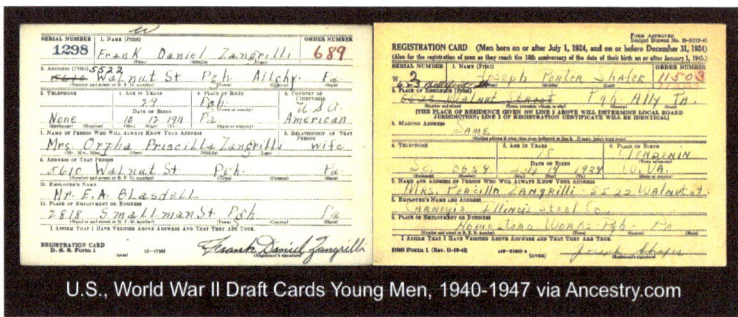

U.S., World War II Draft Cards Young Men, 1940-1947 via Ancestry.com

Zangrilli lived at 5522 Walnut St. and the one person he trusted to always know his address was his wife, Mrs. Orpha Priscilla Zangrilli, who lived at 5610 Walnut St.

Shafer lived at ~~5522 Walnut St.~~ 623 Bellefonte St. and the one person he trusted to always know his address? Mrs. Percilla Zangrilli, who lived at 5522 Walnut St.

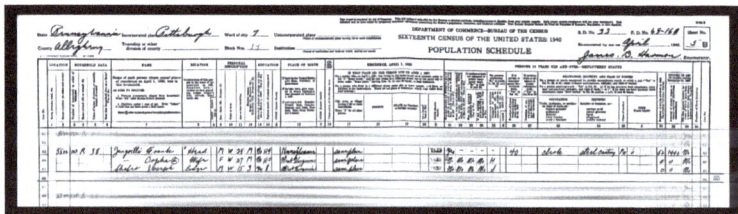

Where, according to the 1940 census, they all lived at the same time.

Honorable Mentions

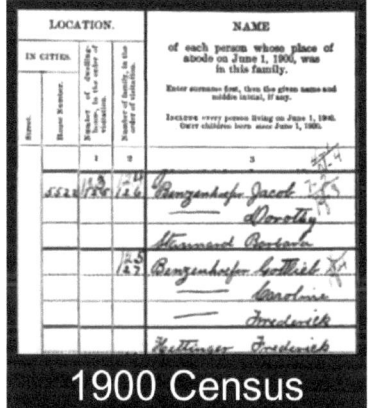

1900 Census

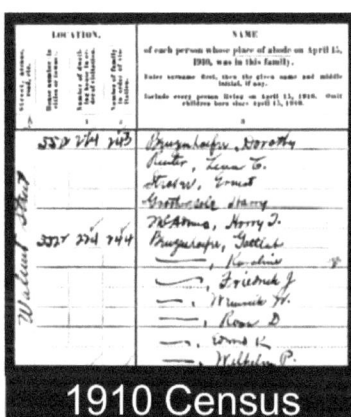

1910 Census

Fred H Hettinger: Lodger, 16 years old, barber, emigrated from Germany in 1891. Nothing else turned up on this person.

Lena C Renter: Lodger, 22 years old, dressmaker (Barbara connection?), emigrated from Germany in 1902. Various name spellings still turn up nothing.

Ernst Strohm: Lodger, 29 years old, machinist, chauffeur, emigrated from England in 1902. Nothing else turned up on this person.

Harry Grothersolr: Lodger, 29 years old, chauffeur with Presste Auto, emigrated from England in 1902. Nothing else turned up on this person. Various name spellings still turn up nothing.

Harry Mcadams: (middle initial is I or J, possibly T?) Lodger, Pittsburgh native, plumber. Nothing else turned up on this person.

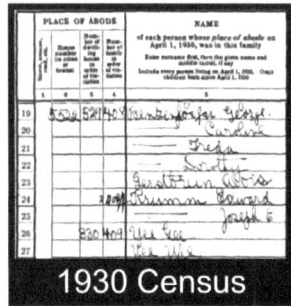

1930 Census

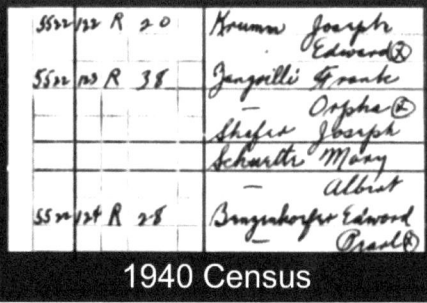

1940 Census

Alois Gerstbrein: Lodger, 55 years old, butcher, emigrated from Germany in 1891. Nothing else turned up on this person.

Gee Yee, (39) and **Wee Yee** (30): Brothers, California natives, owners and operators of a laundry shop. Nothing else turned up on either name.

Mary Schuette: 21 years old and husband Albert Schuette, 34 years old, painter.

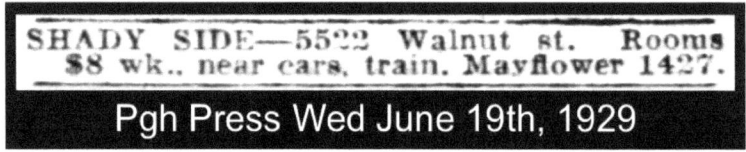

SHADY SIDE—5522 Walnut st. Rooms $8 wk., near cars, train. Mayflower 1427.

Pgh Press Wed June 19th, 1929

A nod of acknowledgement to the 1920s 8$/week lodgers.

Part Three: Commercial History

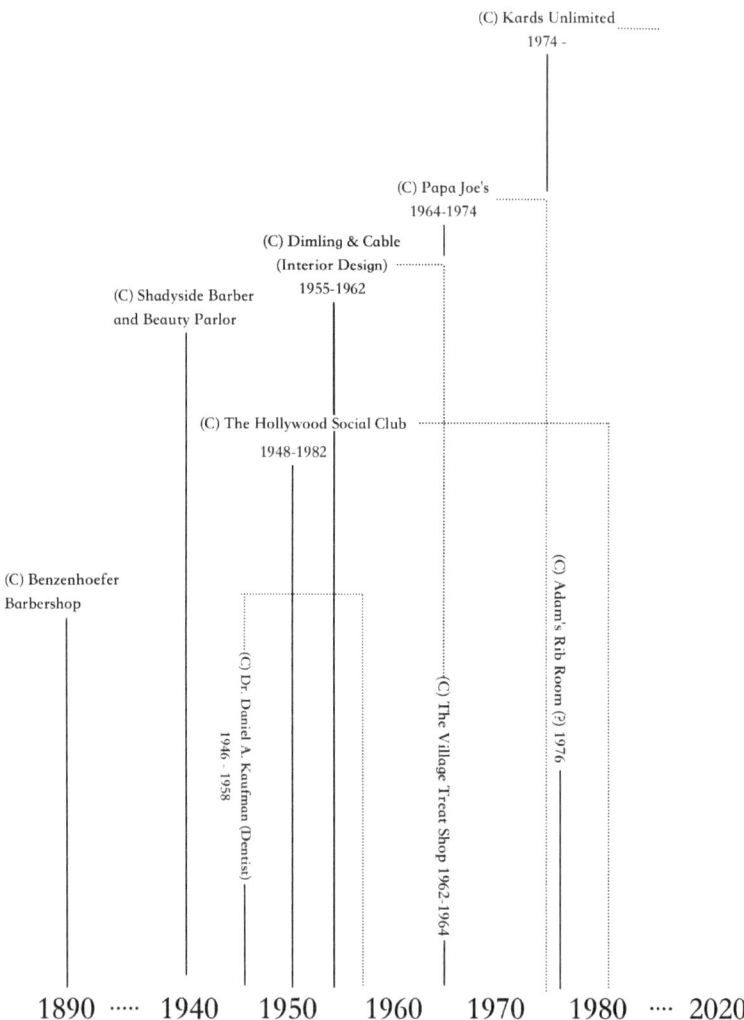

(C) Kards Unlimited
1974 -

(C) Papa Joe's
1964-1974

(C) Dimling & Cable
(Interior Design)
1955-1962

(C) Shadyside Barber
and Beauty Parlor

(C) The Hollywood Social Club
1948-1982

(C) Benzenhoefer
Barbershop

(C) Dr. Daniel A. Kaufman (Dentist)
1946 - 1958

(C) The Village Treat Shop 1962-1964

(C) Adam's Rib Room (?) 1976

1890 ····· 1940 1950 1960 1970 1980 ···· 2020

A note regarding photographs...

Throughout this book are a series of photos. Some of these photos have been archived and unseen since they were developed 40-50 years ago. Some of them were negatives or slides that I digitized. Often these photos were damaged, many of them were in black and white or grainy sepia tones.

While this project is, primarily, one of historical preservation it's also an attempt at historical restoration.

As such, each one of these photos has been repaired, enhanced, and colorized digitally by me over the course of writing this book. Many of these photos are being shown here for the first time. None of this would have been possible without them.

At the end of this book, you will find an extensive acknowledgement of each archive, each archivist, and each photographer who helped in the creation of this journey.

A journey that begins February 19th, 1935, at the corner of Aiken Ave. and Walnut St.

Walnut St. and Aiken Ave.   Feb 19, 1935

Photo source: Pgh City Photographer Collection 1901-2000.

While 5522 remained a home until the late 1940s, by 1935 Walnut St. had become less residential and more commercial. From this eastward-facing view of Walnut St., 5522 is a few blocks forward on the right. Among other places in this photo you can see the original Schiller's Drug sign.

Barbershop, Beauty Parlor,
Patent Article Manufacturer
1893 - 1940

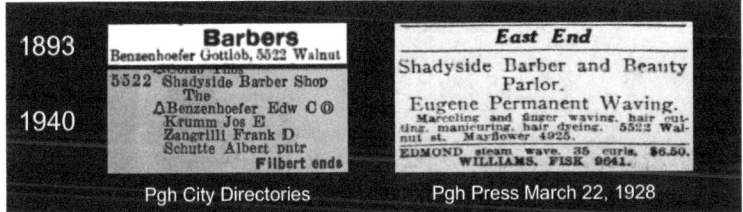

| 1893 | **Barbers** | | *East End* |
| | Benzenhoefer Gottlob, 5522 Walnut | | Shadyside Barber and Beauty Parlor. |

Pgh City Directories   Pgh Press March 22, 1928

It was possible to find references as early as 1893 and as recently as 1940 to 5522 Walnut St. as a barbershop or beauty parlor in some way.

Pgh Press August 1930

In August of 1930, M. Blankenhorn placed four identical advertisements in the *Pittsburgh Press* to announce his company's services as a Patent Articles Manufacturer.

Dimling & Cable Inc. Interior Designers
1955 - 1962

In the *Post Gazette*'s December 12th, 1981 article, "In Search of Good Taste," Arthur Dimling mentions being an avid collector of objects shaped like monkeys. He goes on to say that he has no design philosophy at all but rather, "*guter geschmuck*," which means "good taste" in German. Often he and his partner Charles Cable were known to perform puppet shows for their clients' children who came to visit their shop at 5522 Walnut St. In that same article, one of his students was quoted as saying, "If Dimling's shop hadn't been there in the 1950s, Walnut wouldn't be what it is today."

It seems apparent that this was true for others as well...

While researching Dimling & Cable Inc. I found myself directed to the website 1stDibs.com. This website, among other things, is a place where sellers can auction away art. As I sat staring at this painting on my computer screen, I felt a strange sense of uncanny valley. I knew I was looking at something familiar but it wasn't familiar at all.

The painting was done in the 1960s by artist Fay Moore, and is the earliest depiction of 5522 Walnut St. I was able to uncover. We clearly see the mansard roof described by Emil Sitz in 1890[3].

We also see there are doors on both the left and right, while in modern times there is only one door in the center. We also see alleyways on either side of the building. The bricks on the building to the right are consistent with the Shadyside Theater. However, with the bricks on the left we can see the rightmost side of what was possibly a house at the time with a slanted roof.

I am genuinely proud to say that this painting, as of writing this book, hangs in Kards Unlimited. The painting is home. Carrying the spirit and love of Dimling & Cable back to the halls and walls within which they laughed so many decades ago. Unfortunately, I could find very little information on Fay Moore. I am deeply grateful for their contribution to this project.

---

[3] See page 12 for the December 12th, 1890 *Pittsburgh Dispatch* "Building Record" description of 5522 Walnut St.

Dr. Daniel Kaufman
1946 - 1958

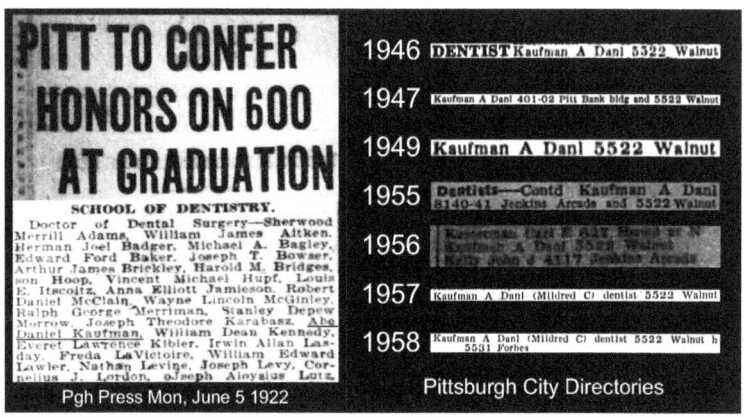

PITT TO CONFER HONORS ON 600 AT GRADUATION

SCHOOL OF DENTISTRY.

Doctor of Dental Surgery—Sherwood Merrill Adams, William James Aitken. Herman Joel Badger, Michael A. Bagley, Edward Ford Baker, Joseph T. Bowser, Arthur James Brickley, Harold M. Bridges, son Hoop, Vincent Michael Hupf, Louis E. Itscoitz, Anna Elliott Jamieson. Robert Daniel McClain, Wayne Lincoln McGinley. Ralph George Merriman, Stanley Depew Morrow, Joseph Theodore Karabasz, Abe Daniel Kaufman, William Dean Kennedy, Everet Lawrence Kibler, Irwin Allan Lasday, Freda LaVictoire, William Edward Lawler, Nathan Levine, Joseph Levy, Cornelius J. Lordon, Joseph Aloysius Lutz,

Pgh Press Mon, June 5 1922

1946 DENTIST Kaufman A Danl 5322 Walnut

1947 Kaufman A Danl 401-02 Pitt Bank bldg and 5522 Walnut

1949 Kaufman A Danl 5522 Walnut

1955 Dentists—Contd Kaufman A Danl 8140-41 Jenkins Arcade and 5522 Walnut

1956

1957 Kaufman A Danl (Mildred C) dentist 5522 Walnut

1958 Kaufman A Danl (Mildred C) dentist 5522 Walnut h 5531 Forbes

Pittsburgh City Directories

As the Benzenhoefer barbershop beauty parlor days come to a close, we welcome Dr. Abe Daniel Kaufman. A 1922 graduate from the University of Pittsburgh Dental School, Dr. Kaufman opened his own office at 5522 Walnut St., where he maintained his private practice for at least 13 years.

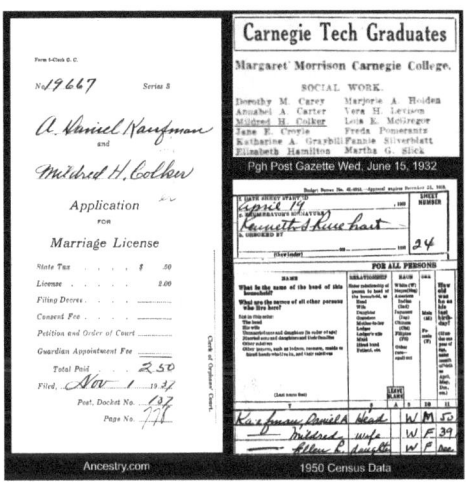

In 1937, Kaufman married Mildred Colker, a 1932 graduate from Margaret Morrison Carnegie College for Social Work. In December of 1949, they had a daughter named Ellen.

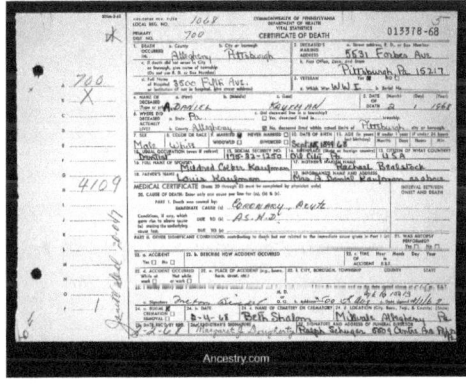

Kaufman died in 1968 and from his death certificate we learn that he was a veteran of WWI.

The Village Treat Shop
1962 - 1964

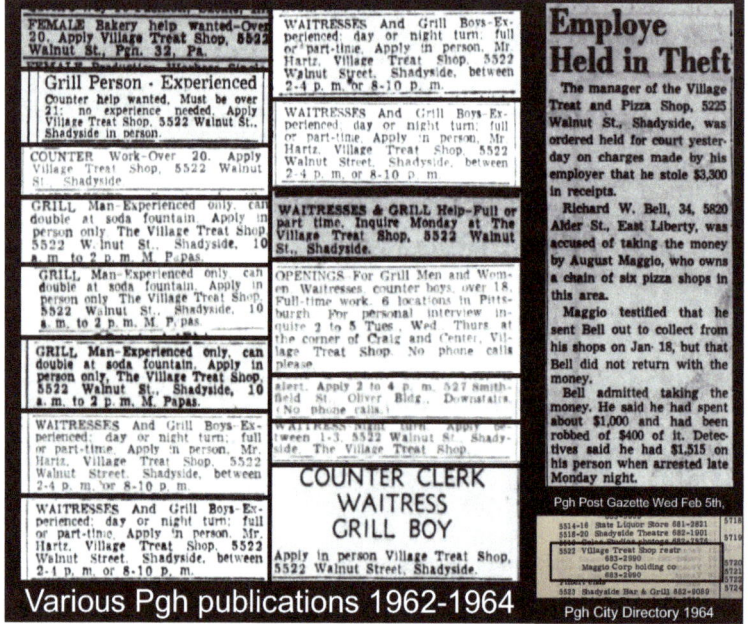

Various Pgh publications 1962-1964

Pgh Post Gazette Wed Feb 5th,

Pgh City Directory 1964

The Village Treat Shop isn't something I can say much about. In 1964 the manager robbed the store of $3,300 and was soon caught. And from these ads we can infer that it was a classic soda fountain joint with a grill that existed as a business at 5522 Walnut St. at least from 1962-1964, and they were always hiring.

Papa Joe's
1964 - 1974

View of Papa Joe's at 5522 Walnut St.   May 4, 1965

Photo source: Pgh City Photographer Collection 1901-2000.

Prantl's Bakery at 5525 & Papa Joe's at 5527 Walnut St.   Circa 1979

Photo source: Marc V. Rock-Steady, Indovina Family

Originally located at the corner of Ivy St. and Walnut St., Papa Joe's moved to 5522 in 1964, at which point Joe's daughter, Jean Cohen, was the owner.

I am not entirely certain where the name "White Hut" comes from. Through discussions in the Friends from Shadyside Facebook group, the general consensus is that they may have been capitalizing on the already established "White Castle" and "White Hut" names. But also, and more likely, it could simply be referring to a "white coffee," which was just a coffee with a bit of cream.

Papa Joe's White Hut   1965

Photo source: Ancestry.com

What I love about these two photos is how much of this building has changed when comparing it to the Fay Moore painting on page 49. The alleyway has been bricked shut. However, upon examination of the side of 5522, the memory of the neighbor's slanted roof and the apartment door remain.

Either way, we can tell from this photo that sometime in the late 1960s they shortened the name, simply, to Papa Joe's.

In 1974, Papa Joe's moved to 5527 Walnut St., where its name remained until 1984, when Jean's daughter, Pam Cohen, and Pam's partner, Gail Klingensmith, took over ownership and changed the name to Pamela's, making it the second Pamela's location, after their first opened in Squirrel Hill in 1980.

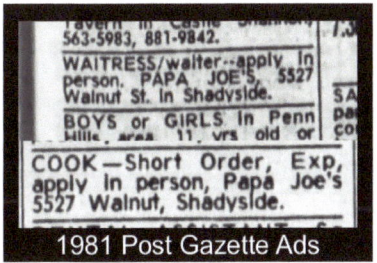

1981 Post Gazette Ads

55

Adam's Rib Room
1976

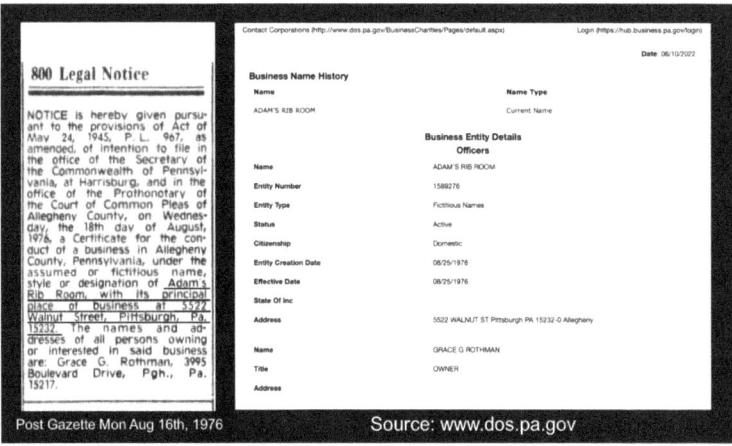

One of my favorite finds is Adam's Rib Room. A fictitious name for a fictitious company that opened at 5522 Walnut St. in 1976. It's a favorite because every time I go asking people about it they simply tell me, "That's when the mob owned the Hollywood Social Club, so I'd leave it alone..."

Either way, I was able to uncover nothing besides these two sources.

The Hollywood Social Club
1948 - 1982

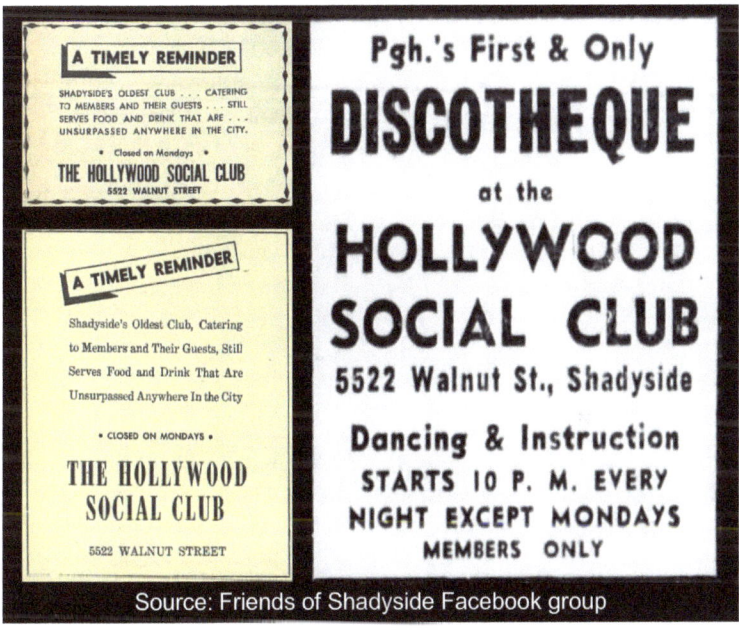

Source: Friends of Shadyside Facebook group

Exactly when ownership transferred from the Benzenhoefers to Blandi was a detail I was unable to uncover. Nonetheless, it is clear that, in 1948, restaurateur Frank Blandi set out to create the Hollywood Social Club.

Unsurpassed anywhere in the city, The Hollywood Social Club would draw in unbelievable decades of celebrity sightings, endless evenings of jazz, the best food Pittsburgh has ever tasted and... the mob.

Newspaper clippings from across multiple archives plus the narrative histories of members from the Friends from Shadyside Facebook group paint an intriguing picture of what this club may have been like.

The club experienced a few burglaries over the years, the first of which happened only a few months after the club had begun being built. Apparently a workman had left a "ladder leaning against the building," which Herbert Flynn used to climb inside, ultimately stealing $281. Flynn, apparently too drunk to realize, had left his wallet at the scene. When police finally found him, he admitted to the robbery and also to drinking $101 of the $281 he stole.

In 1951, they were burglarized of $317 cash and liquor valued at $200.

Then, in 1959, they were robbed of $175 cash and $200 booze. On this date, orphan Bernadette received her first beauty treatment.

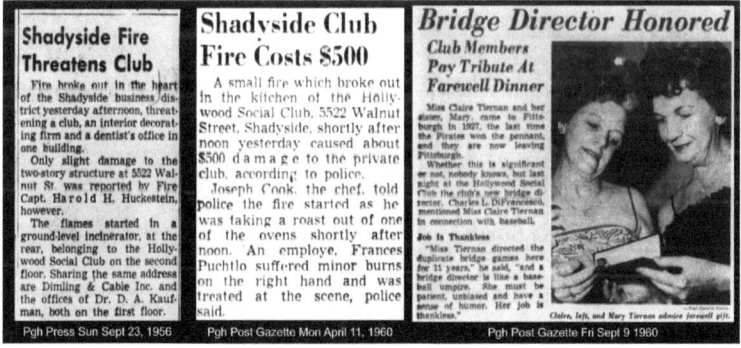

The club had at least two fires, the first in 1956 and the second in 1960.

A decade of bridge games were played at the club's tables.

It is, however, the 1961 and 1964 Golden Anniversary announcements that I am taken by – for I wish to be so lucky as to love and be loved for such a period of time. Congratulations to both the DiNardos and the Perinos on their 50th wedding anniversaries.

I do (often) think, and worry, about this watch.

Now here is where we change it up and begin to see Walnut St. from new perspectives. Here is where stories told in news clippings merge with photography to bring the past momentarily into the relative present.

Here, in 1957, closing out our decade, we catch an uncanny and visceral glimpse of that change. The Hollywood Social Club throws a children's party during The Shadyside Chamber of Commerce festival on Walnut St. A festival captured across several images by photographer W. Eugene Smith.

Scan QR code to be taken to Shadyside Chamber of Commerce Spring Festival and Street Fair 1957!

Shadyside Chamber of Commerce Festival 1957

View from Mobile Gas Station at 5416 Walnut — 1957

Mobile Gas Station at 5416 Walnut St. — 1957

SW View from Bellefonte and Walnut — 1957

Girl Leaning on a Parking Meter — 1957

View of 5411 Walnut St. — 1957

Photographer W. Eugene Smith

Money's All You Need To Drink In Some Clubs

Clubs violating the law against serving non-members, on the basis of The Press survey, included:

Almono Club, 116 Court Pl.; Club 30, 136 Sixth St. (second floor); Young Men's Thinking Club (second floor), 3214 Forbes Ave., Oakland; Abyssia Section Two, 3502 Penn Ave. (second floor), East Liberty; Hollywood Social Club, 5522 Walnut St. (second floor), Shadyside; Lyric Club, 5711 Ellsworth Ave., East Liberty; and South Pacific Club, still in East ...

Of these, Almono, Young Men's, Abyssia and Club 30 served guests long after the designated cut-off time of 3 a. m.

(The upstairs at 136 Sixth St. has an interesting history of after-hour club activity.

rooms were occupying by the

... Lt. Allen Carnahan was wounded with his service revolver while at the bar at 6 a. m. He resigned from the force after the shooting, which involved a woman companion, Shirley Cavanaugh.

Warning ignored at Hollywood Social Club.

Pgh Press Sun Dec 25, 1960

Club Waives LCB Hearing

The Hollywood Social Club, 5522 Walnut St., Shadyside, waived a hearing scheduled here today before a State Liquor Control Board (LCB) examiner.

The club in effect was pleading no defense to LCB citations for sales to non-members and after-hours sales.

The club was one of seven singled out as a liquor-law violator by reporters for The Press after touring the after-hours spots to gather evidence for an article published last Dec. 25.

Pgh Press Tues May 2, 1961

The Hollywood in Shadyside
Liquor Board Suspends Social Club's License

The state Liquor Control Board yesterday suspended the license of the Hollywood Social Club of Allegheny County, one of the most regular gathering places in the Shadyside night life belt.

Eight charges are listed in the board's complaint against the club at 5522 Walnut St. The license suspension begins July 15 and is effective for 90 days "and thereafter until conditions are restored."

However, a licensee has the option of either closing during the suspension term or paying a fine of $10 for each day the board may either accept the fine or put on pressure.

Sets Shortage in Income

The board's bill of particulars alleges that the club: Failed to maintain its by-laws, failed to maintain records in conformity with board regulations; failed to keep for a period of at least two years complete and truthful records.

Further, the board charges that there was an unexplained shortage in the club's reported cash income.

The suspension order goes on to cite the club for admitting persons to membership ...

Cited Over Dues

Furthermore, the club is cited for failing to charge and collect dues from members, and failing to present application to the board for the bond and sidearms...

Other liquor license suspensions in the county were ordered for:

James B. Mato, McKees Rocks, 30 days, color after hours, permitted gambling.

Ralph J. Beasley and Martin Minervik, operators of the Shamrock Cafe, 1510 Penn Ave., Strip District, 10 days. In this case, the board cited the fact that last January Minervik pleaded guilty in Federal Court here to failing to affix a $50 wagering tax stamp.

Pgh Post Gazette Thurs July 2, 1964

In 1960, The Hollywood Social Club got busted for selling booze, after hours, to non-members. In 1961, they pleaded no defense. In 1964, they got their license suspended.

Of these, Almono, Young Men's, Aloysius and Club 30 served guests long after the designated cut-off time of 3 a. m.

(The upstairs at 136 Sixth St. has an interesting history of after-hour club activity.

rooms were occupied by the

... Lt. Allen Carnahan was wounded with his service revolver while at the bar at 6 a. m. He resigned from the force after the shooting, which involved a woman companion, Shirley Cavanaugh.

Here, however, is a coincidence hard to ignore. In the article "Money's All You Need To Drink In Some Clubs" a familiar name and story leapt out at me... Shirley Cavanaugh... the reason why I began doing research in the first place.

But that's not what the Hollywood Social Club was truly about, was it? The golden anniversaries, the robberies, the children's party and bridge: all binding around the edge of a quilt. The fringe, momentary stitches that wander the borders around the larger picture.

This was not the Benzenhoefer's Walnut St. That much is certain. This was Walnut St. in the 1960s. Musical culture and barefoot poet hippies were playing bongos at the coffee shops.

'Exploring' Pittsburgh　　　　　**By Gilbert Love**

Our 'Greenwich Village'

Walnut Street after dark didn't turn out to be quite as Bohemian as I had been led to believe.

For years I had been hearing about unusual goings-on in this Shadyside business street. Coffee houses had appeared and the street had been nicknamed "Espresso Row." Students and others gathered in these places and talked endlessly as they sipped their small cups of strong coffee.

Occasionally, it was reported, a patron would bring a set of bongo drums or a guitar and singing would break out. There were even occasions when the wail of bagpipes filled the air around Walnut and Bellefonte.

More recently I had heard that more beer than espresso was being consumed along Walnut Street. Also the area had gone more "arty."

Visitors reported seeing men with beards and sketch pads . . . girls in sloppy attire . . . sometimes a barefoot poet or sidewalk artist.

I wondered a bit about all this because I had seen Walnut Street occasionally in daytime. Then it was just a nice little shopping district with some unusually fine clothing stores and a scattering of such things as art and book shops. The art and literature fit into the neighborhood naturally because it always had had some real artists and college people in residence.

Street Jumping

To check on the reports I went to Walnut Street last Friday evening with some friends.

It was jumping. Crowds, mostly young, surged along the sidewalks and ebbed and flowed around the doors of places like The Casbah, The Encore and Fox's Cafe.

A man at the door of the Encore told us there wasn't even standing room inside. A glance showed he was right. The place was full of people, smoke and sound.

A crowd stood around the entrance to Fox's, apparently waiting for room to develop inside. A girl who managed to get in stooped at the doorway and took something out of her shoe. "That's her ID card," explained a bystander. "To prove she's old enough. The bartenders are getting particular about that."

We got inside the door of The Casbah and later got a small table against a wall. A trio on a platform behind the bar was playing and singing folk-type music.

A girl in street attire worked her way through the crowd and took our order. Some people standing over us were talking about "in jokes." I didn't discover what they are.

Patrol Cars, Police

There were a few beatnik types on Walnut Street this evening, but by and large its patrons were well dressed. Most of the men were even wearing jackets and ties.

The crowd seemed well behaved, too. Of course, there were several policemen in view at all times, and patrol cars kept working their way through the traffic-jammed street.

Everything considered, I'd say Pittsburgh's "Greenwich Village" is pretty decent, and worth a visit just for fun. If you want to sit down, though, better choose a night other than Friday.

Pgh Press Tues Aug 20, 1963

Harold Betters records *Live at The Encore*, David & Anthony record *Walnut St. Live* at The Casbah.

As for us... well, we cruise into 1965 in style...

"Walnut Street at Night"   May 1965

Photo source: Carnegie Library of Pittsburgh Photo   Photographer: Bill Foster

Night, Walnut St. Laughter and light blare from the Shadyside Theater.

Warning ignored at Hollywood Social Club.

Like moths to beautiful moonlight, we are carried by the sounds of jazz and scents of Devonshires down the block. Arriving at a speakeasy alleyway, we climb an "Everest of stairs" until we come upon a door marked "Members Only."

But no sweat, right? Remember, if you got the money, it's fine...

We ring the buzzer and head inside The Hollywood Social Club. Our coats are checked. Now a walk through the crowd reveals some familiar faces...

Not the least of whom is Rick Maroni, whose wondrous trumpet stylings you might hear upon a Saturday night.

Ric Maroni, the former trumpet player in Johnny Costa's old band, now has his own combo at the Escapade on Monday nights and the Hollywood Social Club on Saturdays. It includes Bob Kress on bass, Danny Varlotto on drums and Ronnie Bickel, the son of Bill Bickel, the long-time organist (now retired) at Johnny Laughlin's Shamrock Room, on the piano. ... Connie Lauar has moved her ticket agency from the Penn-Sheraton Hotel, where it was located for four years, to the Peerless-Willoughby Camera Store at 431 Smithfield Street. The Midtown Ticket Agency will identify it henceforth.

Post Gazette Obituaries May 10, 2008   Pittsburgh Post Gazette Wednesday March 31, 1965

★ ★ ★
After wearing out two of the original Broadway cast albums of "Fiddler On the Roof," Gert and Bill Mazelsky, the Civic Light Opera Company's publicity director, are finally going to see the show itself in New York this week-end. ... The Lenny Littmans have a 20th wedding anniversary coming up on December 28 ... Roland King has resigned as the film editor at Channel 2 . . . The Holiday House's John Bertera was the dinner host to his outgoing star, Kay Starr, and his incoming headliner, Gail Martin, at the Hollywood Social Club on Sunday night.
★ ★ ★

The 22-year-old singing daughter of Dean Martin, of Steubenville, O., where she was born, is the current headliner at the Holiday House and will be through December 17. Miss Martin, a Reprise Record artist, was featured on her father's summer replacement television show this year with Vic Damone. The Day Brothers, a comedy team, are at the Holiday House, too.

GAIL MARTIN

Post Gazette Tuesday December 5, 1967

Or catch the golden trills of Gail Martin's Sunday night serenade.

Birth of cool

After World War II, the place really changed. One sign of its transformation came on a cold spring morning in the late 1950s. Steve Snow, who grew up near Walnut Street and brokered real estate deals there, remembers the moment clearly.

His phone rang at 3 a.m. "This is Orson Welles," said the voice on the other end of the line. "I am coming to Pittsburgh." Welles asked Snow, an old prep school classmate in Illinois, to meet him the next night.

"What are you going to do with me?" Welles asked.

Snow said, "I am going to take you to Walnut Street."

At the time, the street was gaining a reputation as a hot night spot. Welles and Snow had their choice of nightclubs and restaurants.

They started with a few drinks at the Fox's Cafe, a bar at the corner of Walnut and Bellefonte streets.

Later, they walked to the Hollywood Social Club. To get in, they had to squeeze down a side alley, walk several flights and hit a buzzer on the third floor.

Inside, the after-hours club featured a bar that stretched from one end of the room to the other. A back room was full of people, including comedian Henny Youngman. Welles and Youngman spent a few minutes talking and exchanging one-liners. Welles and Snow stayed at the Hollywood Social Club until 5 a.m. or 6 a.m., with the actor catching an early-morning flight out of town.

In the late 1950s and early 1960s, celebrities, local politicians, athletes, attorneys and executives filled the street at night. Among the repeat visitors was comedian Bob Hope, who buzzed through in the 1960s and 1970s. People spotted him with friend Billy Conn, the Pittsburgh prizefighter. Conn would drive Hope around Pittsburgh and often end the night at the Hollywood Social Club.

Once, Ralph Colaizzi spotted Hope emerging from the alley at 8 a.m. Colaizzi owned the building. He didn't speculate on what kept the star so long.

Down the street, the Encore jazz club was playing host to musicians such as trumpet players Roy Eldridge and Yank Larson, trombone player Harold Betters and pianist Earl Hines. Today, Cozumel Mexicana and Victoria's Secret sit on the spot.

People lined up to get into the Encore, according to Carol Rosenbloom. "This wasn't just weekends. This was every night."

In the late 1960s, Willard Shiner opened the Gaslight, a three-story club-style place just off Walnut on Bellefonte that was controversial because of its nude paintings.

Nightclubs were not the only new arrivals. Fashion hit the street, too.

Pgh Post Gazette Sun Sept 26, 1999

67

Or perhaps it's your lucky night and you run into none other than Orson Welles, who, upon a 3 a.m. visit to Pittsburgh, called up his childhood prep school classmate Steve Snow and grumbled into the phone, "I'm coming to Pittsburgh, what will you do with me?" The answer no doubt was: "We're going to the Hollywood Social Club."

Orson Welles

Henny Youngman

Maybe that same night Henny Youngman sits, crackin' jokes across the strings of his violin. Or you arrive one night where suddenly Billy Conn and Bob Hope stumble punch-drunkenly past you in the cramped Hollywood Social Club Alleyway.

Billy Conn

Bob Hope

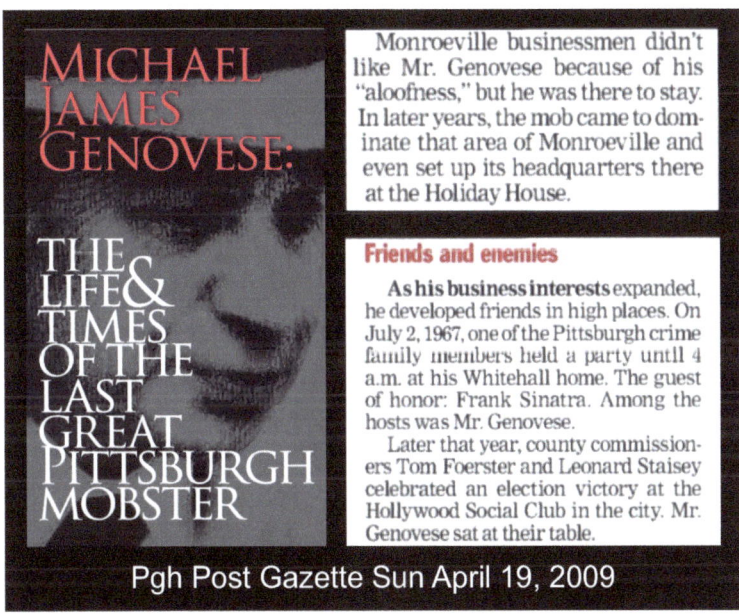

While there does seem to be some sort of connection between the Pittsburgh Mafia and The Hollywood Social Club, I could find very little to support this. Whether it is true or not I can't say. I can only say, with this one reference, that Michael James Genovese "The Last Great Pittsburgh Mobster" was headquartered at the Holiday House in Monroeville and was often seen having dinner with some fairly important people at the Hollywood Social Club.

No matter who you'd run into, one thing was certain: The Hollywood Social Club was really about the food.

While Frank Blandi may have invented the Devonshire, he perfected the Deviled Crab. Or at least that's the way Patricia Goodwin of Las Vegas remembers it...

Cook's corner

NEWS AND LISTINGS FROM AND FOR OUR READERS

KITCHEN MAILBOX
ARLENE BURNETT
PG Tested

Requests
• **Patricia Goodwin** of Las Vegas writes: "I lived in Pittsburgh from birth through the '50s. I would frequent the Hollywood Social Club, an after-hours club in Shadyside. On the menu was Deviled Crab, and to this day I think about it Could any of your readers know the recipe? My palate would be most appreciative."

Pgh Post Gazette Thurs Jan 8, 2004

Arlene Burnett's Kitchen Mailbox in the Cook's Corner section of the *Post-Gazette* in 2004, a full 22 years after the club's closure. Patricia casts a long shot hoping someone out there might still have the recipe for it.

And you know what?

Someone did...

Shadyside club drew celebs, request for its deviled crab

Bob Hope never left Pittsburgh without stopping in for a nightcap. Chubby Checker "twisted" for a plate of veal scaloppine. "Old Blue Eyes" and Sammy Davis, Jr. visited on more than one occasion.

From 1956 to the mid-'70s, the Hollywood Social Club on Walnut Street in Shadyside was one of the hottest night spots in Pittsburgh.

"Pittsburgh Steelers owner Art Rooney, local celebrities and athletes would stop in for dinner," said owner Chuck DiNardo. "We were known for our Devonshire sandwiches (we served about 1,000 a week) and deviled crab."

Which brings us to Patricia Goodwin of Las Vegas, who remembers the Hollywood Social Club's deviled crab: "I lived in Pittsburgh from birth through the '50s. I would frequent the Hollywood Social Club. On the menu was deviled crab, and to this day I think about it. Would any of your readers have the recipe?"

Mr. DiNardo willingly gave us the recipe, and we're delighted he did; this dish is outstanding.

HOLLYWOOD SOCIAL CLUB DEVILED CRAB
PG tested

- ½ cup half-and-half
- 1 to 1½ teaspoons dry mustard
- A few dashes Worcestershire sauce
- Salt and pepper to taste
- 6 slices white bread, crusts removed and cubed
- 1 pound lump crab meat
- Fresh bread crumbs, about ¼ cup
- About ¼ to ¾ cup melted butter, plus more for coating the casserole dish or ramekins

Preheat oven to 400 degrees. Butter the inside of a 1-quart casserole dish or four 7-ounce ramekins (we used a casserole dish). Place the half-and-half in a medium-size bowl. Stir in the mustard, Worcestershire sauce and salt and pepper.

Add the bread cubes and crab, and gently mix until all ingredients are incorporated.

Place the crab mixture in casserole dish or ramekins. Sprinkle bread crumbs over the crab mixture. Drizzle about ¼ cup of melted butter over mixture.

Bake in a 350-degree oven for 20 to 25 minutes.

Broil for about 30 seconds or until crumbs are golden brown. Drizzle 1 to 2 tablespoons of melted butter over the crumbs.

A note from Mr. DiNardo: "We would place the crab dish under an open flame until the bread crumbs turned golden brown. Then we would drizzle additional melted butter over crumbs and serve. This recipe is also good for stuffing flounder."

Pgh Post Gazette Thurs June 22, 2006

Two years later, thanks to owner Chuck DiNardo, the *Post-Gazette* not only ran the recipe in response to Goodwin's request but also took that time to namedrop Chubby Checker, Art Rooney, Sammy Davis Jr., and Frank Sinatra as people one might have found hanging out on some random night at The Hollywood Social Club.

Correction

Last week's recipe for the Hollywood Social Club's Deviled Crab recipe incorrectly said to preheat the oven to 400 degrees. The correct temperature is 350 degrees.

Pgh Post Gazette Thurs July 6, 2006

71

On a whim, in February of 2024, we needed to move something away from the wall on the second floor of Kards Unlimited. This revealed wallpaper from the Hollywood Social Club which I have cleaned up and published here.

Every Cloud Has a Dynamic Lining
(Time to Embrace Change ... Barbara)

Some people are happy with the same old thing

Some people don't like change.

They get over it most of the time, but they certainly do squeal a lot before they adjust.

Maybe you don't fit into this category, but I do. I tend to like things to remain the same as long as possible. A great deal of the reluctance to accept change has to do with age.

I admit it. I'm older and I don't like feeling unsettled.

BARBARA CLOUD

Would Shadyside ever be the same without its Hollywood Social Club? And what about the theaters we've lost? I still mourn the fact movie houses are now on the outskirts of the city or in malls. And the original Nixon Theater being torn down for the Alcoa Building, then the second Nixon giving way on Liberty Avenue.

We will adjust to the loss of Horne's. But hold onto your memories. They are yours to keep forever.

Nobody can change that.

Pgh Post Gazette Tues May 10, 1994

In the 1994 article "Some people are happy with the same old thing," Barbara Cloud expresses an emotional state of being we can all relate to; a fear of, and so reluctance to, change. A longing to remain comfortably cradled within the arms of familiarity.

Asking ourselves, how could the present moment be meaningful without the past? And what about the future? Will this moment have been meaningful to us?

Would Shadyside find the same meaning now that the Hollywood Social Club was gone? Now that the theaters had disappeared?

No.

Walnut St. has always reflected the human experience, an experience best described as seasonal. Clinging to spring or fall will not impede the peak arrivals of summer and winter. But upon their arrival, we would not be prepared. Being sticky with the past ensures anxiety of the present and dread of the future.

Shadyside Arts Festival 1975
Photographer: Tom Doyle

So we, too, must change. With the seasons, we must fall. With the years, we must brush aside the leaves. With the decades we too must emerge like blossoms beneath so much snow.

As the 1960s rolled into the 1970s, Walnut St. changed further and became known for its Arts Festival, music scene, and eateries.

The Lemon Tree Shop and Clay Place stood beautifully at the intersection of Ivy and Walnut Streets.

The Clay Place and The Lemon Tree Shop   Late 1970s

Photo source: Carnegie Library of Pittsburgh Photo Archives   (demolished 1987)

The Music Emporium, Call Me Mister, Yogurt Works, and Mardi Gras sat near the corner of Bellefonte and Walnut.

Call me Mister, The Music Emporium, Yogurt Works, Mardi Gras — Late 1970s

Photo source: Carnegie Library of Pittsburgh Photo Archives — Corner of Bellefonte and Walnut St.

And Kards Unlimited … wasn't where you think it was.

Kards Unlimited
1957/1974 - Present Day

Post Gazette December 1976 ad

Google 2022 Street View

Originally a Hallmark store, Kards Unlimited first opened its doors in 1957 at 5513 Walnut St., where it remained until 1974. Regardless of its location, the ethos remained the same:

Be tasteful, be quirky, be fun, entertain, spread laughter, enliven the holiday spirit, be a safe and creative space for people to visit and shop for new aspects of themselves.

And few knew this better than Clara Herron...

1947 CMU Yearbook Photo

79

Shopping with Polly
1927

Post Gazette Sun Oct 27, 1996

81

Within the first week of the launch of the *Pittsburgh Post Gazette* (August 8th, 1927), a column titled "In the Shops With Polly" began its run.

Originating as a column geared towards the "feminine reader," "In the Shops With Polly" was concerned with the quality and care put into specific products, and was often printed with a complete shopping list infused with comfort, fun, and local eccentricity.

Starting in 1927, the nom de plume "Polly" was penned by a plethora of different journalists, but the Polly that concerns us most us Clara Herron.

Carnegie Mellon University 1947 Yearbook — Pgh Post Gazette Wed Dec 11, 1963

President of Carnegie Mellon University's journalist fraternity Pi Delta Epsilon and Golden Quill award winner, Clara Herron would write as Polly from 1954-1987.

And from 1974-1987, Clara frequently made certain her Polly columns included products from Kards Unlimited.

Shopping With Polly

See Posters, Pots, Prints

Place to go for all the posters is Kards Unlimited, 5513 Walnut St., Shadyside. But Polly got the word that the store will move to a new location just across the street, 522 Walnut St., in a week or so. After the move, the store plans to expand its poster panorama and also include framed art works.

Thurs Aug 8, 1974

Shopping With Polly

Heavy Snows Warming Sale of Mushy Valentines

Bottled Love

Instead of a ship, you can get a heart in a hand-blown bottle for $2 at Kards Unlimited.

Or you can write original love thoughts in "pure" white ink on bright red stationery.

Fri Feb 10, 1978

Shopping with Polly

Doll Houses Number Two

More Than Cards

Kards, Unlimited, Shadyside, is noted for its greetings from far lands, and from the cleverest creators on our shores.

It has a doll house we hear is spectacular. A tiny parcel post package . . . an outdoor rural mailbox, $5. There's 5522 Walnut St.

Fri Nov 18, 1977

Shopping With Polly

Fun Felicitations

Can't ignore the birthday bunch just because it's summer. To a fisherman, send a soft-art "Fat Mail" card that will make a splash — a fat, vinyl fish, with "Here's your Happy Birthday cod," written on attached luggage tag. To anyone, send Old Sol with the legend, "Happy Birthday, Sunshine!" For a sick-abed, or any good egg, send one stuffed, with text: "Keep Your Sunny Side Up!" With mailing envelope. $1.75 each. Kards Unlimited, 5522 Walnut St.

Tues June 24, 1980

Polly Says

COVER ART done by Pauline Ellison for the paperback edition of Ursula LeGuin's "A Wizard of Earthsea" is a full-color illustration in a collection of posters, notecards and prints matted for framing. They're from The Bantam Gallery, new division of Bantam Books, and will arrive soon at Kards Unlimited, 5522 Walnut St., Shadyside.

Sat May 20, 1978

Shopping With Polly

Little Boxes

Tiny In-Tins, saying such things as "Stamps and Stuff," "Baubles, Bangles and Beads," "Junque" and "Pandora," $1, were so popular last year that they've spawned a crop of boxes just a bit bigger.

They're survival kits for golfers, tennis buffs, runners, dieters, cyclists and drinkers.

Each one costs $1.50. Instant chicken broth, a stick-on bandage, aspirin, a wash towelette, are found in tiny packets in each.

Then a tire patch is added for the cyclist, a tape measure for the dieter, salt tablets for the runner.

Kards Unlimited/ 5522 Walnut St./Shadyside/other stationers

Tues Feb 20, 1979

Shopping With Polly

Imagine this!

The Beatles 1983 Song Calendar, $6.95, adds 52 extra days to your year to help you crowd it all in. Beatle melodies "Eight Days a Week," "Help" and "Imagine," nine others are featured on pages headed by color illustrations first seen on greeting cards.

Important Beatle dates are identified each month, and there are quotes from John Lennon and Paul McCartney.

Kards Unlimited, 5522 Walnut St., Shadyside; University Bookstore, 4000 Fifth Ave., Oakland.

Right: Laurie London, 11, models wool throw-over. Left: Eight-day week calendar.

Tues Nov 18, 1982

Shopping With Polly

Survival Kits

Little metal boxes, put together just for fun, are of some use, too. Each holds a packet of chicken bouillon powder, a mild headache pill, a quick-wash towelette.

Then they specialize, with a tape measure for dieters, a tee for golfers, a tire patch for cyclists.

The tiny survival kits each cost $1.50.

Kards Unlimited, 5522 Walnut St., Shadyside.

Tues March 27, 1979

Shopping With Polly

Names that expand

Now you can buy balloons with the name of the birthday boy or girl or the guest of honor preprinted on them. They come in many colors, six to the $1.50 package.

Kards Unlimited, 5522 Walnut St., Shadyside.

Tues June 29, 1982

Clara Herron 1925-2007
Source: Post Gazette obituaries

Polly — the column, not the writer — has gone through many changes over the years, though there was one constant — off and on — for a 30-year period. Her name is Clara Herron.

Herron recalls taking over the Polly beat from Genevieve McSwigan ("she was from the family that owned Kennywood"). "It was 1954 or '56 when I started to write it, because she was ill."

Herron figures she stopped being Polly around 1987. But she continued to shop, adding "Best Bets" to the Et Cetera column.

"One of the first things I ever wrote up was that spray whipped cream, Quip," recalls Herron, 71, a retiree. "It was brand new. The reason I remember is that I never cooked then; don't now. My mother cooked a pumpkin pie for a [wedding] shower, and I took [the whipped cream along]. I shook it, sprayed, and it hit the ceiling."

Post Gazette Sun Oct 27, 1996

Polly – Clara – an unsung hero of early Kards Unlimited fanfare, concretized in the archives of the *Pittsburgh Post-Gazette*.

How many people read her column, I wonder, to find some new, lovely thing reviewed and worth the trip down to Kards Unlimited. The last two Polly columns I found were written by a different Polly and as far as I can tell – Polly stopped writing entirely in 2004.

Kards Unlimited
A Modern Legacy

Sue Giltenbooth

KARDS UNLIMITED EST. 1968

As mentioned, Kards Unlimited first opened in 1957 at 5513 Walnut St. Its modern legacy, however, began in 1968, when the business was purchased from Hallmark by Sue Giltenbooth, who went on to operate Kards Unlimited until 1972.

At that point, ownership was transferred to her daughter, Mary Sue (left), and son-in-law, Ralph Colaizzi (below).

Mary Sue Colaizzi   Mary Sue and Ralph Colaizzi

Pittsburgh Post-Gazette

Magazine

TUESDAY, SEPTEMBER 25, 1990

ET CETERA

New shop in town

On Oct. 1, Counterpoint, in Loot's former space at One Oxford Centre, creation of Mary Sue and Ralph Colaizzi, will offer contemporary and traditional accessories as personal and corporate gifts. Each piece will have been chosen for quality, design, beauty and function. Designers include Aldo Rossi, Robert Venturi, Achille Castiglioni, Richard Sapper, Ettore Sottsass and Philippe Stark. The Colaizzis are already upbeat. They own Kards Unlimited and Ways and Means, Shadyside; Fan Mail, One Oxford Centre; Flying Colors and Paper Mill, Station Square; and Essex, Oakland. They also brought Department of the Interior to Pittsburgh, the upscale furniture store at the late lamented Motor Square Garden, East Liberty.

Pgh Post Gazette Tues Sept 25, 1990

Scan QR code to be taken on a walking tour of Walnut St. in 1982!

Soon thereafter, the Colaizzis purchased the building at 5522 Walnut St., and in 1974 moved Kards Unlimited into its modern location. Quickly, the Colaizzis became known and respected for their business acumen and soon came to be the owners of multiple businesses in and around Pittsburgh: Ways and Means, The Paper Mill, Counterpoint, and Kards Unlimited, for example.

W View Walnut St. "Ways And Means" on right · 1982

Photographer: Art Steinmark

87

Then, in 1994, ownership transferred to Kristen Kershner, Mary Sue and Ralph Colaizzi's daughter – the irreplaceable and indescribably rad woman who owned and operated Kards Unlimited from 1994 until 2021, with her equally as rad husband, Scott.

Pgh Magazine May 1998   Kristen and Scott Kershner

Few individuals, let alone couples, are as generous, empathetic, genuine, and caring as these two. The legacy this family has created is one of light reflecting through decades of Pittsburgh hearts emanating joy in return. I'm grateful to know them.

Ralph Colaizzi with current owner Amanda Blair

Then, in 2021, after 15 years of being an employee, ownership was transferred to my wife, Amanda Blair, someone whose heart remains dedicated to the unique treasure that Pittsburgh has, since 1957, known Kards Unlimited to be.

She is also someone who purchased this business during a global respiratory pandemic...

But while proverbs say crisis is both equal parts danger and opportunity, Amanda Blair saw this time mainly as the latter. Throughout the early stages of the pandemic and, with the help of web developer Melissa Morrill and her Kards Unlimited staff, Amanda set out to create a website that would aid in relieving the difficult doldrum of the daily quarantine faced by so many Pittsburghers. For months, Kards Unlimited staff delivered books, puzzles and games to anyone who needed them but couldn't leave their home.[4]

---

[4] In the very early stages of the pandemic I would drive puzzles and books to people's homes and make a little clowning show for the kids in the windows. I would get out of my car and put on bright yellow dishwashing gloves and a mask and make a big goofy deal out of using Purell and some sanitizer spray on the packages. I got a few joyful chuckles through a few lonely windows so it was worth it.

CityPaper PITTSBURGH

April 29, 2020

Popular Shadyside novelty shop continues to sell puzzles, cards, and gifts through pandemic

By Lisa Cunningham

How has the pandemic affected Kards Unlimited?

The pandemic has affected us as I'm sure it has affected many other non-essential small businesses who had to close their doors to the public. We've had many sleepless nights and an incredible amount of anxiety, not only for the future of the shop but for our staff. We very quickly turned our attention to an online platform and painstakingly learned (still learning) how to build a functional website. I have literally been building day and night for weeks, stopping only to eat and sleep. ... Our manager Adam Marthens has been going in by himself a couple days a week to get orders together for no-contact pickup and shipping, and Kristen has been busy replying to customers who reach out to us on social media, email, or who call and leave a message. ... We have made so many new best friends while chatting with customers, it is the silver lining of all this.

If all goes according to plan, Kards Unlimited hopes to follow Gov. Wolf's guidelines and reopen the physical store on May 10 with safety measures in place (required masks, one-way aisles, and spots marked on floor for shopping with distance) and plans to begin offering free local delivery. In the meantime, they'll continue to sell items curbside ("distant high fives and thumbs up are shared with no contact pickup") and provide shipping for out-of-towners.

It is a strange place for me to be, here, at the end of this book, trying to keep it simple. When I look at the contrast between 1890s newspaper clippings and 2022 Google searches, I keep finding myself rambling down a long written road about my feelings towards my wife.

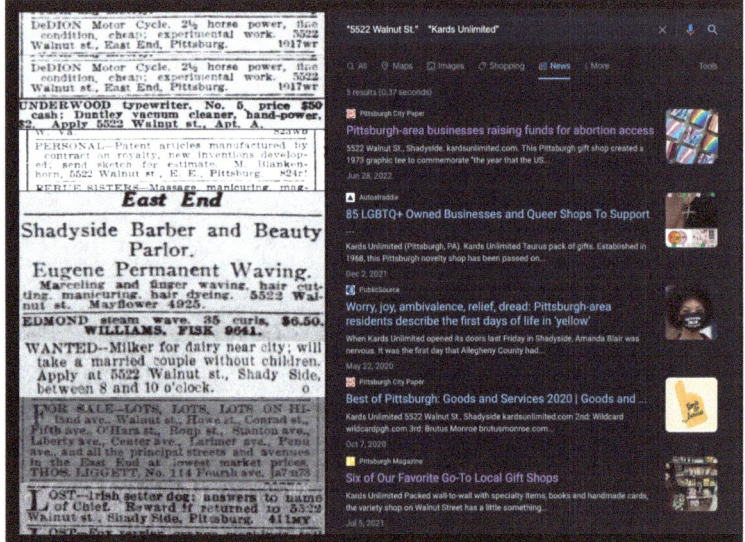

How could I not?

How can I, her husband, not have something more in-depth to say?

I did. I said it. It's this book. If you are, or anyone is, here reading this line, you have made it through a quest of love. I wrote this book to be closer to my wife.

It worked.

At the end of this book, the current state of 5522 Walnut St., here in July of 2022: Kards Unlimited is being awarded Best Local Card Shop in the Pittsburgh Magazine 2022 Reader's Poll.

How fitting.

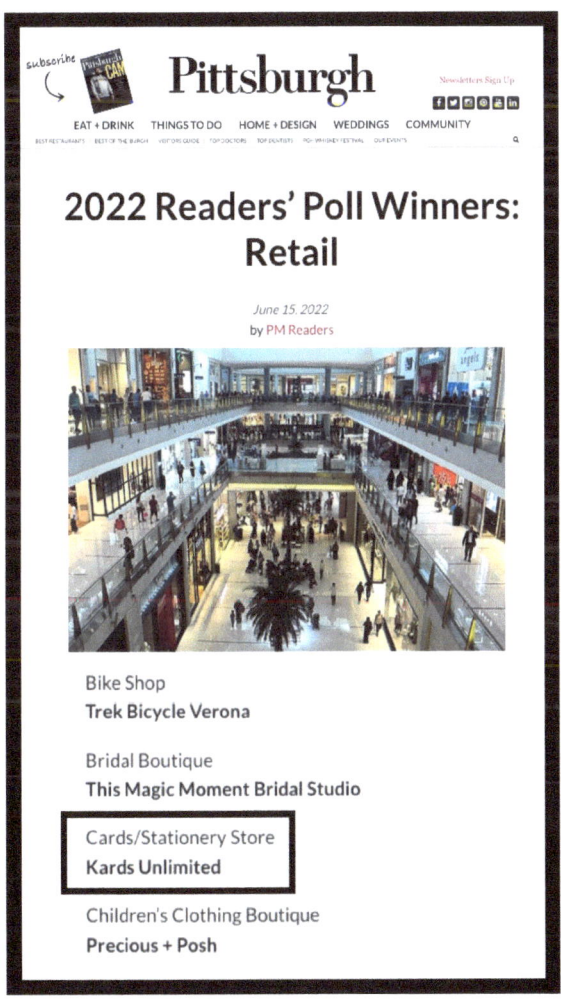

Amanda Blair, owner of Kards Unlimited 2022

Photo: City Paper Photographer Jared Wickerham

Amanda Blair.

Current owner of Kards Unlimited at 5522 Walnut St.

Afterward

Now what?

Now we grow and change again. We face crises as opportunity and opportunity as growth. We slough off the sepia tone of the past. Repair the broken parts of our photographs and upscale the stories told within them. We make sure to always keep coffee and family close by. I wonder what kind of future waits for Kards Unlimited, and Walnut St. to discover it.

I look through all of my photos collected along this journey and can see the change happening throughout time. Where the Lemon Tree Shop and Clay Place stood at the intersection of Ivy and Walnut Streets is now a large, brick, development. The same as where The Music Emporium, Call Me Mister, and Yogurt Works sat on Bellefonte and Walnut – both gas stations are gone. The movie theater is now a Lulu Lemon.

I think of asking all of the same questions that Barbara Cloud asked, but I know the search for any kind of answer is silly. The wheel turns. We are seasonal creatures. Change occurs out of our control and nothing can remain the same for very long.

I think I like it that way.

I think I want to leave it on a simple note.

Love spans the change of eons, let this book be a pause in space time.

Jason Kirin

Amanda Blair and Jason Kirin at Kards Unlimited 2022

Photo: Shady Ave. Magazine Photographer Sean Stipp

Acknowledgements

This project was meant to be simple, uncover a non-modern photograph of 5522 Walnut St., restore it, frame it, present it as a birthday gift, and move on. Well, here we are. A simple restoration turned into months of work digging through the archives of Historic Pittsburgh, the Carnegie Museum, the University of Pittsburgh Library, Chatham University Archives, the Heinz History Center, the Shadyside Chamber of Commerce, Ancestry.com, Reddit, Carnegie Mellon University Library, and few special collections provided to me by individuals I either met through Facebook or had already known.

Each of these archives revealed unique treasures causing profound connections and impressions.

However, it was the Facebook group known as Friends from Shadyside that provided (and continues to provide) the most help in the creation of this book, the videos and photo restorations.

A few members in particular I need to mention...

Mark B. Morrow: who, in order to help identify the chronology of these photos, would comment on the year, make, and model of, literally, every car in every picture.

Paul Corbett: a member who brought a camera along with him to an Arts Festival and the Pirates' win of the World Series in 1979, both being celebrated on Walnut St.

James William: the original Walnut St. historian. His photos, postcards, menus, and memorabilia still hang in the basement of Cappy's for everyone to see.

Judy Conroy Saldi: sent me the most stunning photo of her aunt and uncle on their wedding day in 1955 standing on the sidewalk on Walnut St. In the comment section of this photo, she and her cousin recollect, together, their love for their aunt.

Walnut St. E View outside 5526   1955

Photo source: Judy Conroy   2022 Photo Restoration: Jason Kirin

Marc V. Rock-Steady: an already good friend of mine, Marc sent me a message saying he'd found a box of slides marked "1970s Walnut St." Marc is a member of the Indovina family line. The Indovinas had a fruit market on Walnut St. in the 1940s. These slides were all pristine and beautifully reflected a few 1970s days on Walnut St.

I have never developed or scanned slides before. I had no idea what to do with them.

I tried a flatbed scanner. I took a photo of them over a light box. None of these were satisfactory.

None of these created the quality I required.

I found a gadget from Magnasonic that would scan any kind of slide and any kind of negative, turning them into digitized photos within seconds.

The quality imagery it produces overwhelms any expectation I could have had.

The scanner allows me to scan each slide at multiple exposure levels which is really convenient because when I layer the multiple exposure levels together in Pixelmator I get to toggle the light and color in every which way I want.

Then I give them new skies in an app called Motionleap.

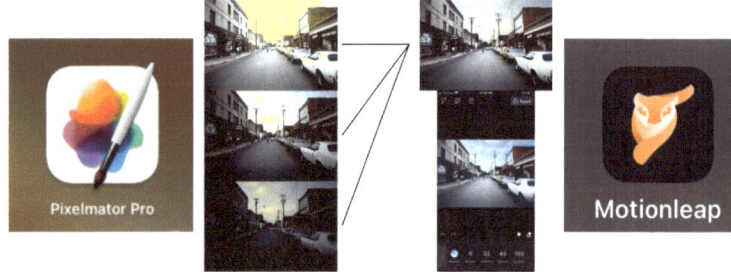

Amira Badran Lopes: A dear friend whose grandmother grew up on Ivy St. and was fond of taking pictures of the early-1900s 5th Ave. mansions. Amira allowed me to scan all of the photos from this fragile album. Some of these photos are Shadyside Churches and also of 5th Ave. mansions that are no longer there.

3rd Presbyterian Church

Church of the Ascension

Hostetter Residence 5th. avenue

Home of Dr. J.W. Anderson

Art Steinmark: mailed me an envelope of 20 black and white negatives. The photographs were a series he took of two of his friends in 1982, walking up Filbert St., coming out onto Walnut St., and chatting in front of Kards Unlimited for a while. Art and I sent messages back and forth for a few weeks, deciding on how these photos should be presented. We came up with the 1982 walking tour of Walnut St. featured in the Kards Unlimited section of this book.

Tom Doyle: an absolute trip and one of the coolest people I've met along this journey. Through the Friends from Shadyside Facebook group, Tom sent me a message letting me know I'd want his photos. Back in the 1970s, he lived at 5509 Walnut St. 2nd floor. Tom was a photographer and his whole thing was "people of Walnut St." With Kards Unlimited behind a perpetual blind spot he'd hang out his window all day taking pictures of people. Yelling down and inviting them up for a joint and a laugh. Tom's pictures are truly amazing, and while a few of them are in this book, the rest of them are in the Facebook group. We still often text each other and occasionally he'll stop in at Kards Unlimited to show me some new negatives he uncovered, or to tell me some story he remembered.

Lisa Marie: While doing research, I turned to Facebook and began to search for people named Benzenhoefer. Interestingly, I found two groups on Facebook dedicated to the name itself. The first group was "Benzenhoefer Family Tradition" and the second was "My Last Name is Benzenhoefer." So I decided … why not … and joined both groups. I explained my presence and purpose, and was soon put in touch with Lisa Marie: The Great-Great-Granddaughter of Gottlieb and Caroline Benzenhoefer.

Lisa, it turned out, was already heavily invested in Benzenhoefer family research and was authentically excited to talk to me about what I was working on.

After many conversations, we became online friends from afar. She lives many states away.

One day Lisa texted me and asked me to call her. She was so genuinely excited when I got on the phone – "I was going through my research files and I found a printed AOL email from 2007 and I <u>have</u> to read it to you!" Lisa told me and then proceeded to read.

As I listened to her … I quickly understood her excitement. The email was from one Benzenhoefer to another and described, in detail, not only visiting Kards Unlimited and being given a tour by the previous owner, Kristen Kershner, but also what she remembered from being a child in her "granddaddy's barbershop."

And what she remembered were beautifully unique and vivid memories about floorboards, sauerkraut, and stairwells.

In other words ... the email was written in 2007 by someone who spent time in the *original* home at 5522 Walnut St. when they were a child.

Here is the email, truncated to omit irrelevant information.

Lisa would explain to me, "For context: the author of the email is the daughter of Freda[5] and granddaughter of Caroline and Gottlieb. So, in the email, Mom = Freda, Granddaddy = Gottlieb, Caroline is by name, so I don't know why she doesn't call her Grandmother or something."

You mentioned abt yr son & wife going to Ellis island and looking for family there. From the lttle that I know, the Benzenhoefers (Benzenhaefers) came first to Economy which is near Pittsburgh and was part of a religious group. They came and then returned to Germany and then came back and again went to the Economy settlement. I sort of think it was called Harmony at one time. I went to visit once with Mom and Aunt Dorothy and we went also to the house where they lived and granddaddy hadhis barber shop in Shadyside. It is now a card shop and I was there twice. It looks like the woodent floors in the shop are the same—well, I was too small to remember the floors when they lived there, but the floors look old with very wide boards and the last time I was there about the year Mom died, the lady in the shop let me peek into the basement where Mom said Caroline would always have a vat of sauerkraut going. Bill Steele remembers more of this cause he is older. I was only 2 when I was there when my grandparents were alive. The shop lady let us go up to the 2nd floor, but no higher cause the upper floors were too broken. The 2nd floor was basically all one big space and destroyed because there was a nightclub there after my grandparents died. I heard Frank Sinatra and such used to hang out in it. Anyway all that was left was this beautiful staircase, wooden, sort of darkwood like mahogany that went up frm the 2nd to 3rd floor. Doris remembered that staircase cause on the 3rd floor my grandparents lived and Aunt Ann and Uncle Fred lived on the 3rd and Doris said every day Caroline would start from the bottom of the staircase and clean it and Ann would start from the top and they would meet in the middle and sit down for a chat.It's a nice story. My grandfather learned to be a barber at Economy because everyone there had to learn a trade. My grandmother came to Pitts at 18 yrs old. She was from close to where my grandfather was raised in Germany but they did not meet until both were in Pitts. Mom said Grandma's 1st job was for theHJ Heinz family as a nanny. I saw once the church where my grandparents were married but I have forgotten the name of it.

Monday, May 21, 2007 America Online

---

[5] See page 22

Dana Kaufman: Thank you for doing yet another fantastic editing job.

Archivist / Archive Acknowledgments

Carnegie Museum: The Carnegie Museum archivist Gil Pietrzak uncovered the photo of the Kards Unlimited storefront at 5513 Walnut St. after it had been buried in a folder since it had been developed.

The Heinz History Center: Kelly George, a Project Archivist at the Heinz History Center Detre Library, was absolutely instrumental in some of the finer details of this project. Through multiple back-and-forth emails, she led me to all of the tools necessary to access, search, and understand census data. She led me to Polk's City Directories and spent an afternoon searching through a few decades worth looking for any listings available for the Village Treat Shop and Benzenhoefer's Barbershop. She also helped me understand the huge map collection available at the Detre Library.

Chatham University Archives: Molly Tighe, archivist who fully understood my project as soon as I reached out to her regarding George Gibson. While we still have yet to uncover a further connection between Gibson and Chatham/PCW, Molly continues to dig and continues to send me photos she uncovers from the archives. Photos that connect Chatham to the greater Shadyside area.

Indispensable Websites:

ArcGIS.com
HistoricPittsburgh.org
Retrographer.org
Newspapers.com
Ancestry.com
MyHeritage.com

Digital / Online Archive

Drawing from the multiple archives mentioned I was able to uncover roughly 100 non-modern photographs of Walnut St. spanning 1935-1985. Throughout 2022 I spent much of my time focused on restoring these photos.

Why I have decided not to include most of them in this book is…

When each photograph was restored to a quality I felt comfortable with, I would post it to the Friends from Shadyside Facebook group and just watch. I'd comment and enter into dialogue with people who actually lived within those moments. People who actually lived within these photographs!

Every time I posted a photo, the comment section would explode before me. Scores of stories poured in; people reminisced about what it was like to work in these places, what the people were like who loved and lived there. The commonality was how much they cared about being there.

As long as Facebook remains, so too will these stories, these real moments explained by the genuine humans that lived them. That is their posterity.

A few restored images of buildings I soon learned were cherished locations demolished by developers in the 90s. People hadn't seen these buildings since then. People hadn't felt these feelings, been flooded with these memories since then either.

In that frame of heart, and mind, people commented on these photos. Those comments moved me. Often to elation. Most often to gratitude. I could find myself there. In these photos with these people! The supplemental material provided by this community through the comment sections of these photos is, I feel, essential for the full experience and exploration of them. So in that community is where the digital museum of Walnut St. shall remain.

The physical museum however... the art and photos regarding 5522 Walnut St. can only be found by exploring the shelves of Kards Unlimited. You'll find the Fay Moore painting there, Art Steinmark's photos there, and also a few other goodies I won't spoil.

Here are a few ways one may access the Friends from Shadyside / digital museum.

- Go to the following address: www.facebook.com/groups/581787848508196/
- Or login to Facebook and search for the group "Friends from Shadyside"
    - In the "media" section of the group you will find the entirety of images I have uncovered from the archives above.
- Or Scan this QR Code

So that is where these photos will be viewable, in the community that produced so many of the originals – coupled with the stories and memories connected to them.

Visit the stories, take them in, read and engage in the comments. They are a wonderful community there. If Facebook is inaccessible to you, email me and I'll link you to the Google drive album.

Lastly, the digital museum is an organism. It will grow continuously. Please feel free to reach out to me at ShadysideHistory@gmail.com if you have any photos or material regarding Shadyside you would like to have restored, colorized, etc. and added into the archives.

Jason Kirin

5522 Walnut St. Residential and Commercial Timeline

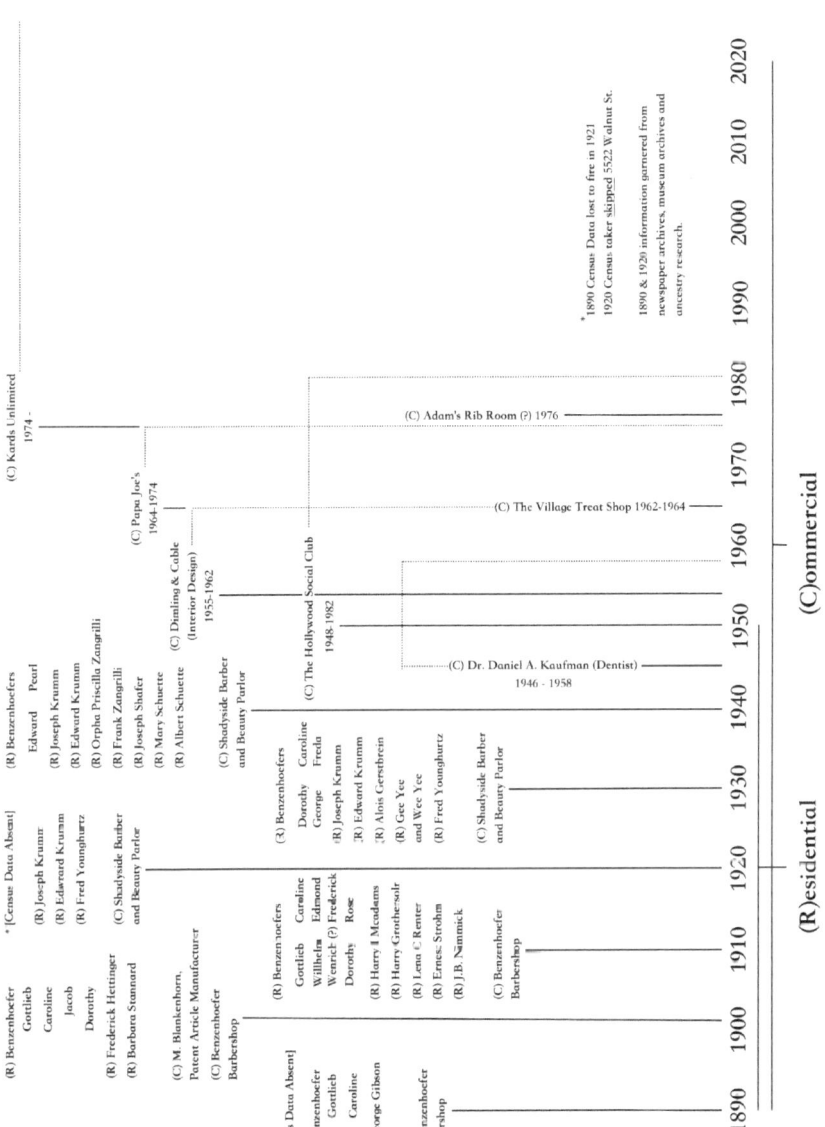

(R)esidential

(C)ommercial

Contact and Social Media Info

Email Contact: ShadysideHistory@Gmail.com
- My second book "From the Furnace, with Love," is an exploration into the multi-generational influence of Shirley Cavanaugh, a 28-year-old sex worker whose testimonies against corrupt Pittsburgh police brought about the total dismantling and collapse of the revered 1950s Vice and Narcotics Squad. Someone who happens to also be my grandmother.
- My love and obsession with local histories and research has grown exponentially since these two books. As I work on further historical collaborations, feel free to contact me about inquiries.

Facebook Pages:
- https://www.facebook.com/FromTheFurnaceWithLove
- https://www.facebook.com/FriendsofShadysideShadyside[6]

Hashtags:
- #FromFarmlandToCardShop
- #FromTheFurnaceWithLove

---

[6] This is not a typo.

Endnotes

Part One: Early History

[1] "Whiskey & Soda." The Lafayette Escadrille, thelafayetteescadrille.org/whiskey-soda.

Part Two: Residential History

[1] US Census Bureau, Census History Staff. "January 2021 - History - U.S. Census Bureau." Www.census.gov, www.census.gov/history/www/homepage_archive/2021/january_ 2021.html.